FINDING TAKASHI

Finding Takashi

CHŌKŌDŌ SHUJIN

LEGENDBOOKS

2023

LEGEND
BOOKS

Edited by Constantin von Hoffmeister

ISBN

PAPERBACK: 978-83-67583-60-2

HARDBACK: 978-83-67583-61-9

EBOOK: 978-83-67583-62-6

www.legendbooks.org

"The testimony of the dead is multifaceted, and their
voices are audible to those who would listen."

— Shōhei Ōoka,
The Battle for Leyte Island

I

Issen Gorin

"YOUR LIVES are worth one ren, five sen. A fucking postcard. At this point in your lives, you will speak only when spoken to. Address me as 'Sir!' When you leave, I am still 'Sir!' Do you understand? You, there, private…"

"Akutagawa, sir."

"Ah, Second Class Private Akutagawa. The son of that dead poet?"

Meekly, the young draftee nodded, his large, cold eyes downcast.

"Ah, don't you go chasing after every whore in Korea like that father of yours. Do you hear me?"

"Yes, sir."

"I can't hear you. We don't have much use for your tea house bullshit here, private."

"Yes, sir!"

"Private Akutagawa, if you make it out of here without cracking up like that old man of yours, if you survive this prelude to hell, you can chase every whore on the Korean peninsula for all I care. If you make it out of here, you'll be a living bullet, a prophet of death. They'll fear that pathetic little carcass of yours. I'll have your pathetic ass praying to fight. You'll beg for combat. You'll make it out of here a warrior, a weapon, but for now… Look at you, you're pitiful! You are the scum of the earth. A father like that… You're ritually impure. You hate me, don't you, private? Insulting your old man like that. You're angry."

"No, sir."

"Louder."

"No, sir!"

"There! You're not even human, less than a man, and too timid to even be considered an animal. At least animals fight back! What did those whores ever see in that pathetic father of yours? Ah! But, my boy, there's no discrimination here. You do hate me, I imagine. I stand for everything your father railed against. You resent every single word I say. Like your crazy father, you must be dissecting each and every syllable, private, like a goddamn haiku. Good. You're no different than the rest of these unwashed bastards. Descended from the shogun's tea master, the son of Japan's most famous pacifist, king of the aesthetes. Yes, you must hate me. You must think I'm some pathetic commoner having a go at the old order. Go on, say it."

"No, sir."

"Ah, finally playing the part of a man, then…?"

The student draftee was silent, owing both to Confucian politeness and to his own fear, recalling the earlier sting of a bamboo cane against his shins.

"So, private, you're not a man?"

"I am a man, sir."

"Finally, out with it! A man, with all the strengths and failings of these stupid bastards around you. Your father was a communist, no, private?"

"My father despised politics, sir."

"A pity he saw fit to slander General Nogi, then. Well, now, you and all these other student draftees are entrusted to my care. Regardless of how pitiful you may be, I am tasked with training all of you to the best of my ability. You, private, present a special challenge! Still, I must transform all of you into fit, disciplined, and proud soldiers, completely devoted to the soil of your birth and loyal to your noble lineage. Yes, you, private. I will demand of all you men the utmost dignity of performance, but I will demonstrate such action by my own example. I'm no hypocrite. Yes, you men will be held to the highest standard. So long as you're in my care, consider yourselves on trial for your fidelity to the Empire of Japan. Until you deploy, welcome to hell."

* * *

Second Class Private Takashi Akutagawa did not go to hell. Neither did he have the option to retreat into the peace of his memories, for time severs the threads of fond emotion in ways that mere distance cannot. Memory, meanwhile, reduces reality to simple abstraction. The present was nothing if not concrete... Takashi had departed Japan; somehow, on the deck of the battleship *Yamato*, polished to the sheen of gunmetal, he was certain that he would never again see the landscape of the homeland that was so indifferently becoming steadily more distant from his field of vision. A steely wind swept over the deck of the ship, painting the landscape the color of dampened ash. Flags of white and red dotted the retreating dock, much like innumerable floating lanterns held aloft by thin strings. The faint strains of jaunty music echoing over choppy grey waters called to mind memories of his younger brother's piano playing; soon Yasushi, too, would be the recipient of a red postcard declaring his conscription, although presently the high school student stood on the dock beside their mother. The forty-three year old widow had been given reason enough to weep, and yet she had refrained, ever dignified. Hiroshi was absent.

The Sunday of November 28, 1943, Shōwa 18, was especially dreary, the mountainous clouds moving in a low and ominous formation. The air was chilled but not yet frigid. Perhaps two hundred other men dressed identically in olive green crowded the ship's deck; indeed, Second Class Private Takashi Akutagawa appeared wholly indistinct from the rest of them. Uncertainty shrouded his fragmented thoughts, and he felt only a nervous electricity. He was a soldier, certainly, and of the lowest rank at that. His health was poor. Beyond that, definitive truth seemed scarce. Tearful women and bright-eyed children in the throng that had gathered as the ship left the safety of its dock for the seas spanning the distance between Japan and the Korean peninsula had taken no notice of the red insignia bearing a solitary star on the collar of his freshly laundered uniform. They had remained content, instead, to brandish their flags and cheer as patriotic anthems were played over a loudspeaker, weeping as much from sorrow as from patriotic fervor for these youthful emissaries of the rising sun. The men in the crowd, meanwhile, most of them older than his father had been at the time of his death, had shown naked flashes of what could be described as either envy or apprehension in their eyes. Emotion be damned, all of their forms were swept away by the rain as the *Yamato* made its way through the Tsushima Basin, further and further from Honshū in the direction of the Korean peninsula.

From time immemorial, wars have been fought by those perhaps most ill-equiped to fight them, and waged by those lacking the depth of perspective to agonize over their deaths.

Upon embarking, Takashi had consecrated his body to Japan and to the emperor, and he had boldly sworn that in doing so, he would bring with him no regrets. In the brief span of his twenty years, he was burdened with no firmly held regrets. This was due to neither action nor inaction on his part, only to the opaque sanctitude of youth.

"The entire nation with a united will shall mobilize its total strength so that nothing will miscarry in the attainment of our war aims..." Two years prior, these words had been broadcast via radio, written by the Shōwa Emperor and spoken by the prime minister, General Hideki Tōjō. The bombing of an American naval base had accompanied this pronouncement of war in December. Soon, all manner of essays on the matter had appeared in the papers, hastily composed by everyone, from housewives to acclaimed dramatists, some of whom he was personally acquainted with, invariably accompanied by images of patriotic destruction, almost sublime in the scope of its fury.

"Don't be fooled by appearances — this photo, more than anything else, is an honest representation of of a scorching hell engulfing some thousands of men," the critic Hideo Kobayashi had written in an editorial he'd chosen to title "War and Peace," which bore no relation to either Tolstoy or to any sort of Christian torment. The photo in question had been an image of a battleship engulfed in plumes of swirling grey. Drifting smoke consumed its broad deck; though no flames were visible, it was apparent that the vessel was filled with flames. Implosion would shortly become explosion. Beside it, another ship was capsized, its hull gleaming like a steel torpedo beneath the sun. The waters that bore them were streaked with oil with the salience of blood, soon to be ignited. Streaks of jagged flames would soon dance upon the surface of those Pacific waters, the same ocean whose translucent waves lapped upon the shores of Japan. The Imperial Japanese Navy had condemned those men to a hellish demise.

Second Class Private Takashi Akutagawa was the grandson of Major Zengorō Tsukamoto, a decorated naval officer who had been a casualty of the siege of Port Arthur during the war with Russia. The *Hatsuse*, the third *Shikishima* class battleship, was sunk by a Russian mine during the Japanese effort to block the port of Lvshun on May 15, 1904, Meiji 37. The *Hatsuse* was stationed at Port Arthur, covering the landing of troops, but she struck a mechanical mine. She signalled for help, but soon struck a second mine, sealing her fate. Three hundred crewmen were saved by torpedo boats, but at least four hundred men drowned, most of them officers sacrificing themselves to save their men. Major Zengorō Tsukamoto, too, quite likely saw those blinding flames resembling hell before his death; by all accounts a brave man and a model soldier, he had gone down with his ship, perishing at the age of thirty-four, leaving behind a daughter nearly too young to retain crystallized memories of him. Takashi had met neither of his grandfathers; his paternal grandfather, Tōshizo Nīhara, had succumbed to the Spanish flu three years prior to his birth. Rumor had it that as the old businessman had been on his deathbed, his only son had been in a geisha house, seeing off an Irish friend who was soon to set sail for his homeland. Yes, as the cruel old man lay dying, his son had been in the company of five or six geisha. That was what Takashi's father had written, at least. His father, the acclaimed writer and poet, had been summoned from his revelry to see his dying father, the source of much childhood trauma, in his final hours.

"The battleship with the hoisted flags has come. Everybody salute! Banzai! Banzai! Banzai!" the old man had evidently shouted in a fit of senile delirium, despite having never served his nation in any capacity of note. Meanwhile, all that his son recalled was the reflection of the moon atop the mirrored surface of a hearse. Ryūnosuke Akutagawa, inauspiciously but proudly christened with his mother's noble surname, rather than that of his father, had recorded this in a brief missive entitled simply "Death Register." The piece was elegiac in its austerity. Less than a year before his own death, the illustrious writer, essayist, critic, and poet had coldly described the deaths of his mother, elder sister, and father with piercing detachment. Takashi felt little fear when, upon reflection, he was brought to the realization that he would soon join the ranks of those in the Akutagawa family death register, *Tenkibo*. This did not cause him despair, only a sense of grim resignation. He'd had a sort of premonition that he would not survive this war; any army who saw fit to draft this frail student of French and English literature, only recently having recovered from a recurring bout of pleurisy, would surely be abortive in whatever mission it sought to undertake. More than anything, Takashi had wanted to become a novelist, and in service to his country, his passion had been deferred with a stupefying finality. As though fevered, as a man facing certain death, Takashi had written several short stories and numerous poems before beginning what the army described as spiritual and physical training, much like the "Spartan discipline" that his father had received as a child.

"To the utmost limits shall I go on to write. If what I am writing I do not write now, I do not know whether I shall ever write it!" His father's words, as well as those of Kyokutei Bakin, resounded in his heart, and he, too, had momentarily become lost in the frenzied nirvana of fiction. Now, that floating world was eternally distant.

"Open your hand to the clenched heart

What is the pitiful bloody thing that terrifies without that power?

If it wasn't the only thing I took from my chest..."

On February 17, 1941, Shōwa 16, Takashi's brief modernist poem had been printed in a small journal edited by a prominent figure in the Tokyo literary scene; his eldest brother, Hiroshi, had encouraged him to publish the avantgarde piece he'd written shortly before receiving notice of his conscription. The lyric composition, nearly acoustic in the sparse quality of its verse, had garnered comparison to the writings of his father, who was posthumously ranked as the leading figure of the Taishō literati, the namesake of Japan's most prestigious literary award, the Akutagawa Prize. Even so, these days, much of his father's writings were censored; assorted autobiographical pieces, written at the end of his life in the confessional style of the I-novel, escaped such vicious editorial butchery. Many of these brief vignettes revealed a sensitive affection for his young sons, as well as an almost morbid fear for their safety.

"And so Takashi finally eluded death. When he had begun to fare a little better, I thought about writing a sketch of the events surrounding his stay in the hospital, but I decided against it because of a superstitious feeling that if I let my guard down and wrote such a thing, he might relapse. Now, though, he is asleep in the garden hammock. Having been asked to write a story, I thought I would have a go at this. The reader may wish I had done otherwise."

Takashi's father had written those words in July of 1923 following his young son's tenuous recovery from a stomach ailment. Precisely four years later, Ryūnosuke Akutagawa was gently carried to voluntary death by poison, the conclusion of his life punctuating the end of the Taishō era. "Ryū-chan," he and Hiroshi had called him, rather than "papa." The youngest brother, Yasushi, had not known him long enough to call him anything at all. Unrelated to his father's depiction of his childhood illness, Takashi was, indeed, haunted by a sense of doom, his private sword of Damocles. Much like his father before him, he lived beneath the shadow of hereditary madness.

"He barely made it through each day in the gloom, leaning, as it were, upon a chipped and narrow sword."

Confessing his sins in a brief autobiography titled after Dostoyevski that more resembled a poetic suicide note than anything else, Ryūnosuke Akutagawa had first encountered visual and auditory hallucinations at the age of twenty, he'd written; tormented by schizophrenia, he'd had visions of semitransparent cogwheels accompanied by migraines and flashing lights. Takashi, having only recently crossed the threshold of his second decade, had been party to no such metaphysical torment, and yet his fear of such things persisted. Nor was he permitted to sleep peacefully in that forgotten garden hammock in Tabata as he'd done as a child, shaded so gently beneath leaves of vivid green. War was something removed from either logic or madness, he thought, set apart from both reason and lunacy. Takashi had gone from the dormitory at the Tokyo School of Foreign Languages in Fuchū to those cramped and humid army barracks; a perhaps excessively introverted young man, both experiences in education were miserable for him. His disposition was far too individualistic to function with any degree of ease in such communal environments, especially taking his failing health into consideration. He related some of these vignettes to his elder brother stationed at the air force base in Chōfu, often in verse so as not to attract undue attention to their correspondence. This idea he'd taken from the writings of his father's government-sponsored sojourn throughout China from March to July of 1921. Takashi lived under the assumption that he would soon face similar disillusionment, although much like his father, he held no animosity regarding the populace of the occupied territory whose soil he would soon traverse.

Officers and student draftees alike found cause to slander Takashi's famously pacifist father; his maternal grandfather, the war hero, was apparently no longer relevant; invoking the name of Major Zengorō Tsukamoto accomplished precious little in the way of personal defense. His father had once written an account of General Maresuke Nogi that was less than a hagiography, alongside pithy aphorisms denouncing Japan's aggressive militarism in one of his newspaper columns... His father had died in 1927. Despite this, these writings had ensured that Takashi was treated especially poorly. "Some honor... We're going to our deaths. Then again, if you can buy a life with honor and a salute... That's some bargain." Hobbled by politeness, Takashi was powerless to either defend the name of his father or to purchase any degree of respect from his impassioned compatriots. His cold deference bought him merely ridicule.

"Don't crack up like that lunatic father of yours..."

"The greatest service you could do for Japan would be to kill yourself like your old man. At least we wouldn't have to worry about hauling your dead weight around Korea!"

"Your dad saw his doppelganger? Thank God we don't have to put up with two of you...!"

Takashi had endured each of the insults with a haughty stoicism. This was due in far greater part to an excess of self control than to a lack of anger on his behalf. His father had written dozens of tales of great warriors who died heroically in battle; meanwhile, Takashi could see himself as little more than a sullen, antisocial poet damned to walk in the shadow of a man greater than he.

"Next to war, crime, rooted as it was in private passion, was almost understandable. But war meant one's duty to the Emperor, and nothing else."

— Ryūnosuke Akutagawa,
'The General'

Some Men Meet
Their Shadows

TABATA, in northern Tokyo, now Kita, is situated beside an upward slope, sheltering much of it from the sun and painting the landscape in shadow, the vivid green hues of its sedate hillsides appearing as though filmed through a lense of honeyed sepia. The enclave is marked by subdued ridges and old-fashioned gardens dotted with Shinto shrines and small altars to Jizō Bosatsu, the Buddhist deity said to protect children and travelers. These statues were often swathed in red scarves and accompanied by small towers of coal-colored stones that had been stacked by neighborhood children or their superstitious grandparents. Takashi and his brothers had once piled up stones in such a manner, albeit haphazardly, always smiling. Presently, there was no need for such sentiment. The Yamanote line continues to run alongside this place that could be described as a vestige of Shitamachi, that final refuge of old Tokyo, once Edo, whose grass is sometimes painted blue by shadow. To this day, Tabata is known as the artists' quarter, housing poets, actors, painters, and a host of souls who see fit to defy convention in a calm manner, respectful of the ancients even in their defiance of an increasingly repressive society. As a child, Takashi recalled climbing trees with his father and Hiroshi on the lawn surrounding that modest suburban home. His mother, cradling their baby brother, Ya-chan, in her arms, looked on. The tall, handsome writer, thin as a reed and dressed in a fine summer kimono, climbed a withered tree to chase after his small son, who soon reached the sharply arched roof, breaking into a run along the glazed ceramic tiles. Hiroshi, always the star… It had been an especially warm July in 1927. Four or five years later, in that suburban two-story house in Tabata, the portrait of a dead man adorned the old-fashioned parlor, a malingering Taishō holdover. In the left corner of that room facing the still unpaved street, the painted eyes of a melancholy man gazed forward, just as cognizant of the space surrounding him as he had been at the end of his unhappy life.

"It's uncanny…" Yasushi had said, redirecting his sight from the painting to his oldest brother, who was dressed in a smartly tailored student's uniform with gleaming brass buttons; Yasushi, meanwhile, was too young for such a smart garment.

Takashi, attired much like Hiroshi in his uniform of heavy black twill, took advantage of this. "Doesn't it look like his eyes are following you?"

Yasushi's eyes remained fixed on the painting, while Hiroshi looked on, apparently bemused but silent.

"He's too old to be Hiroshi, but it's Hiroshi's face…"

"So, he can watch you in the future, too."

Situated in the armchair in the corner, Hiroshi wore a smirk reminiscent of their father; upon viewing this, Yasushi glanced once more at that melancholy painting by Ryūichi Oana, who was trained in the school of Cézanne and served as their surrogate father. Takashi continued, "Hamlet saw the ghost of his father, too, you know."

"That's a lie! The ghost was a fake."

"Or so he said…"

"That painting… It's Hiroshi?"

"It sure looks like him, no? As you said, it's uncanny."

Clasping his dimpled hands over his large eyes, little Yasushi ran from the room. Once it was certain that he was far from earshot, both of his brothers laughed. Their mother's soothing voice could be heard in the adjoining room. An abrupt shift to sharpness in the tone of her voice suggested that she heard their laughter.

* * *

The landscape of Takashi's childhood receded from memory much like the panoramic view of his homeland that soon became indistinguishable from the steely blue waters of the sea. The infantrymen on the transport ship, roughly 3,500 who had been headquartered in Nara, near the old capital of Kyoto so beloved by his father, and presently en route to be garrisoned in Seoul, hailed from throughout Japan.

"The objective of daily life in the army barracks is to perfect the self-discipline of the soldiers through military drill."

Prior to their departure, the young recruits and student draftees, none of them having yet reached the age of twenty-five, had been forbidden from reading books, periodicals, or newspapers without having obtained explicit approval from their commander. Writing fiction, then, was certainly out of the question, as was Takashi's perusal of the avantgarde poetry of Stéphane Mallarmé and Jean Cocteau that he had so often sought to emulate; quite successfully, he'd proudly admit after a decent amount of saké; his French was now to be used only for the purpose of translation. Art had been traded for utility, as it were, and the creation of beauty was curtailed for the proliferation of what was described as a glorious national essence. Meanwhile, Hiroshi, now an aspiring actor who had trained at Keio University in Minato and who presently remained stationed in western Tokyo, was being trained as a mechanic for Yokosuka planes. The factory conditions had led to his having become tubercular, his letters implied. Even so, being the eldest son of a famously widowed woman, it was readily apparent that Hiroshi was not to be sent to his death unless the mainland of Japan faced imminent threat. Takashi harbored no resentment for this privileged position held by his brother; indeed, their intermittent correspondence was one of his sole sources of relief, and he wanted little more than to do right by him. Hiroshi was married, too, and Takashi saw no need for there to be another Akutagawa widow.

In basic training, a fresh recruit was often ordered to stand at attention for hours, remaining motionless no matter the weather, forced to appear as though impervious to whatever insults his drill instructor saw fit to pelt him with. When either the agony of stillness or superficial wounds to his youthful pride became too great, he would collapse, promptly receiving a strike across the shoulders with a bamboo cane. The young man's willpower and self-discipline were at fault and needed supplemental cultivation, he would be told in a clinical manner. His superiors would be on constant watch for any potential flaws in his erudition, temperament, and bearing. The barrage of trivial questions was incessant.

"You had time to eat, private? Then surely you had time to clean that rifle."

"Did you have time to sleep last night? Yes? Then, surely you had time to polish those boots!"

Takashi, prone to a ruthless sort of insomnia that was exacerbated by the banality of his present circumstances, often felt compelled to make a sarcastic remark, but he refrained on every occasion. Obsessive by nature, he found it deceptively easy to fixate on his own silence. This earned him a certain amount of respect from his superior officers; indeed, being tall and fine-featured, he was the very image of a model soldier, appearing as though having posed for an army recruitment advertisement. Naturally, this earned him only scorn from the enlistees who surrounded him, most of them rough young men from the countryside.

Over a year had elapsed since Takashi's conscription; the time that had since transpired had been filled with an emotion too muted to be described as anger, but it was certainly of an essence nonetheless tinged with violence. Try as he might, he could not place a name on this lucid sincerity that was forever retreating from his grasp.

Certainly, there was a beauty to this half-formed sentiment that lacked sufficient passion to be given a description of any substance. Despite repeated attempts to use his intellect to understand these thoughts, this spirit of conflict, he was ultimately defeated. His resources thoroughly depleted, he recalled so many words exquisitely crafted with the express intent of stirring passion within the hearts of impressionable young men. Language had been weaponized, it could be said, and yet he could not deny the beauty in the words of Hideo Kobayashi, the critic who had famously lashed his father's corpse.

"…now that the war has begun, your precious life is no longer your own. As long as you take your life from Japan and there is a war in progress, you are not free to do with your life as you please — even should it be in the name of mankind."

Takashi had few concerns regarding the name of mankind. He could not say that it had been purely the words of another that had caused his compatriots to regard him as suspect; inferior, even. He could very well say that his own father's words were the reason for their ill will. Had Ryūnosuke Akutagawa not been so outspoken in his disdain for war, Takashi Akutagawa's own timid presence might have done little to arouse the latent animosity that would have launched itself at whatever stimulus invited its caustic attention. Even bearing this knowledge, Takashi could not find cause to resent his father. His life was no longer his own from the moment of his birth: he could no more resent his father for having caused his existence than he could resent those elegantly manipulative words for being the source of his torment. Existence, itself, was painful, and he was not granted the latitude to extricate himself from it. In a morosely amusing satire that his father had penned mere months before dying, a certain passage was especially foreboding: "I do not wish to be born. In the first place, it makes me shudder to think of all the things I shall inherit from my father — the insanity alone is bad enough." Takashi had inherited a vicious talent from the man widely regarded as one of the greatest intellects known to Japan, but he was spared the hereditary madness, so far as he knew. He had passed the age at which those ominous visions and sounds had first begun to haunt his father. The words and actions of others, the external, were what presently threatened him.

"In a day that will surely come, the Japanese words through which Japanese culture and politics are carried out will become a kind of terrible and heavy burden. This complicated language will certainly abort Japan's modern politics, but the political expression that begins in the world of Japanese language will, unless there appears an unimaginable genius, come to nothing at all."

Yojūro Yasuda's words seemed prophetic. Since the beginning of the war, Takashi had seen language twisted in ways both too deftly subtle and arrogantly overreaching for the masses to comprehend with any degree of cohesion. His intellect only served to torment him. Due in equal parts to opacity and artificially sparkling prose, society had fallen into a quagmire of half-truths. The average man lacks the introspection to grasp his capacity to be manipulated; more than anything, this was apparent. A convergence of words and history had enticed the populace into a comfortable state of fearful hatred towards a manufactured enemy, its threat artificially inflamed. Words were presently designed to become actions. Over seventy million subjects of the Shōwa Emperor were expected to go to their deaths should the enemy invade Honshū, becoming ichioku gyokusai, shattering like precious jewels and fighting until the very last, joining their deceased loved ones in glorious national suicide. Far from eroding their beauty, death would only serve to immortalize it. Was this, then, a national immolation?

Presently, Japan possessed one of most well-trained armies and, beyond that, one of the most sophisticated navies in the world. Warring states had given way to a war against the very logic of humanity, as though a string had been pulled that unraveled the peace that had earlier been so tenuously maintained. In the span of less than a century, a nation of feudal warlords had modernized with frightening speed under the guidance of the Meiji Emperor, ably joining European nations in the manic rush for creation of empire. Previously isolationist, Japan began its foray into colonialism by taking Manchuria, Taiwan, the Korean peninsula, the Philippines, enclaves of China, and most recently Burma. Vastly underestimated by the West, Japan had established itself as a major world power, losing its mind in the process, Takashi's father had written in a rare moment of political critique. This was a land driven mad by the vicious workings of both modern societal upheaval and modern warfare. General Nogi's bloody victory at Port Arthur nearly forty years ago marked the first ever Asian defeat of an "enlightened" nation.

"One of my sons gave his life at Nanshan and the other at 203 Meter Hill. Both of these positions were of the greatest importance to the Japanese army. I am grateful that the sacrifice of my sons' lives was in the capture of such important positions, as I feel the sacrifices were not made in vain. Their lives were nothing compared to the objects sought."

This was the reply that General Maresuke Nogi had given to the Russian General Stoessel upon hearing his condolences. By all accounts, Nogi had afterwards collapsed in tears, driven nearly to a nervous breakdown by the merciless mechanisms of modern warfare and denied permission by Meiji himself to die by seppuku and assuage his shame with the honor only possible in a bygone era. Takashi could not help but wonder what his father would think of his own potential death on foreign soil for a cause he would undoubtedly find reprehensible. Surely, he would have sympathy for his twenty-one-year-old son dressed in khaki and smoking rationed cigarettes.

Shame could be described as seeing oneself as though through the eyes of those around him, a vision of the self reduced to a third-person experience. There is a requisite soberness for shame to manifest. To realize that one is no different than all the rest, even when thrown into the hell of introspection… That, alone, was the source of Takashi's shame.

"Under the influence of the weather, even the gods lose their reason. 'Let's exterminate mankind! Let loose the ravenous dogs!' was the cry that resounded from the heavens to the depths of the Sea of Japan and made it rage in all directions."

— Sōseki Natsume,
The Heredity of Taste

III

Shikata Ga Nai

"RYŪNOSUKE AKUTAGAWA, what do you have to say about the death you decided upon, yourself? We, the living, are relieved to imagine you drifting in a faint, peaceful light beyond the veil of death. My friend, sleep peacefully. If we should dare be as wise as you, we should do our best to ensure you don't feel ill at ease as you sleep. We will continue to pray for your deceased soul; you can rest in peace. The sadness is that you're gone… Ryūnosuke Akutagawa. Your friend, Hiroshi Kikuchi."

A light rain had been falling on the morning that Takashi's father succumbed to gentle death by poison. The summer had been unusually warm, Takashi still recalled, even as the autumn wind now chilled his thin shoulders. Beneath the sharply arched rafters of that graceful Buddhist temple, which took upon itself the gravity of centuries, Takashi had been seated beside his brother Hiroshi. The boy of seven had been named after the speaker, Hiroshi "Kan" Kikuchi, an esteemed playwright and his father's friend since their school days. Alongside such promising young writers as Masao Kume and Yuzuru Matsuoka, Kikuchi and Akutagawa had revived the failing literary magazine *Shinshichō* with their translations of the writings of Anatole France, as well as their own neo-realist poetic stylings. Then the same age as Takashi, the student draftee, his father had used the pseudonym Ryūnosuke Yanagikawa; this, Takashi assumed, had been done out of

19

introversion rather than from any sense of shame; he had famously despised familial voyeurism.

The low headstone at Jigan-ji Temple no longer gleamed when bathed either in sunlight or in moonlight; its surface had long since taken on the softened quality of grey velvet, more resembling a cushion than a grave. The scent of moss permeated the shaded grounds, even beneath the sun. That day near the end of July, the *Shinshichō* writers had once again gathered. Ashamed of his own tears, Takashi had nonetheless been witness to grown men weeping without reserve.

A shimmering of heat —

Outside the grave

Alone I dwell.

Sunset aboard a ship is entirely distinct from the setting sun viewed from even the most picturesque of continental vistas. From every conceivable angle, light engulfs the vessel in a blinding feat of visual immolation. Like the flame of a freshly struck match, brilliant gold gives way way to a saffron hue nearly liquid in its glory; beneath it, deepest blue reflects the dawning night sky. The sun, that immortal disk of distant flame, disappears beneath the broad horizon of the west as the moon is enthroned, alone, sovereign in the darkness.

Takashi, a poet by blood and by nature, was given few opportunities to recount his appreciation of such violently beautiful imagery these days. Perhaps this was for the best; it would be a tragedy for such beauty to be reduced to the realm of the mundane, the everyday. Even so, as the sun made its departure, he was inexorably surrounded by the obliteration of daylight, even as the strain on his nerves persisted. A pity, for this was no place for the composition of poetry or the contemplation of the sublime.

While a fair percentage of the officers serving in the Imperial Japanese Army were of either aristocratic or samurai lineage, most of the enlisted men were culled from the ranks of commoners.

Hiroshi, too, was now an officer, having entered the Maebashi Army Preparatory Officer School in Gunma Prefecture as a candidate for Executive Class A. No doubt his status as firstborn son had sealed this fortuitous position. Upon graduation, he was stationed at the maintenance corps headquarters for the 244th Air Squadron. Takashi, then, due to both his noble lineage and his rank of Second Class Private, was something of a curiosity. While he was loathe to cast a uniform net of judgment over all of his superiors, he could comfortably testify that a plurality of them saw in him some strain of weakness; perhaps this made them resent this hereditary delicacy presently within their own hearts, even if it was fortified by their smartly tailored regalia. Takashi served as a conduit for the exorcism of their private self-loathing.

Japanese military training capitalized on existing tradition and historical legend; custom and superstition were weaponized to mold a fighting man willing — no, grateful — to go to glorious young death for both his nation and, moreover, for his emperor. He was to think of nothing beyond the dignity of Japan. Such a death could only be regarded as his highest duty. The eternal concept of "death before dishonor" had been pushed to a frightful crescendo, and its reverberations threatened to shake the very foundations of both society and sanity.

"The NCO's birthplace should be the company; his growth is also with the company; and his place of death should also be with the company," so said the Bureau of War Ministry.

Even the bolt-action Type 99 Arisaka rifle that Takashi had been issued bore the imperial crest. A cruel irony, as his own family crest, that ancient seal so elegantly chiselled atop his father's low stone grave in Jigan-ji, was that of the prime minister, the 5-7-5 paulownia blossom. Poetic, even in death. Apparently, Takashi's drill instructor had said, the emperor had graciously seen fit to issue this pathetic specimen of man a rifle. In resigned silence, Takashi questioned the emperor's judgment; he'd decided against remarking that the emperor must, then, truly share his father's talent for poetry.

* * *

In his weekly newspaper column, "Shuju no Kotoba," Ryūnosuke Akutagawa had once compared soldiers to children. He loved the heroic attitude and the so-called glory; he marveled at it, even, perhaps to the point of envy. Now, there was no such need for Takashi to mention this, for everyone around him had already read it with the intent of detecting some sort of insult to arm themselves against him. His father, himself a martial artist of some prowess, had ably demonstrated respect for mechanical training, and had at length described the value he placed on a certain sense of animal courage which he had apparently lacked. It was a courage bolstered solely by faith, and thus could exist even in the midst of even the most unscrupulous massacre. This phenomenon was only present within the hearts of children and soldiers, he'd written; only they could simultaneously gaze into a torrent of ruin caused by outside forces and maintain any degree of faith. Like children, too, when flagging, that primal faith of soldiers could be heartily roused by trumpets and military songs, regardless of the reason for their fighting, and they would bravely, happily confront any enemy with indefensible courage. It mattered not what would await them beyond the fortress they took. Conquest was its own glory.

Therefore, his father said, soldiers boast. They boast of their courage; they boast of the beauty of the homeland for which they fight… Like the artist describing his painting, like the novelist describing the plot of his most recent work of fiction, soldiers boast, equal in justification to the writer or the artist. Moreover, when their missions of creation or destruction prove successful, soldiers are permitted the honor of wearing medals, much like the writer or artist whose works are festooned with the praise of greater names than his.

Naturally, the angry young men who surrounded Takashi took umbrage at this. Had his father's works not been assigned in various school curriculums, they would have never known the surname Akutagawa and would have simply regarded Takashi as yet another vain Edoite with an old-fashioned name. His brother did not seem to suffer for this; the fervent Shintoists in Chōfu likely regarded that ancient name with undue respect, and so Hiroshi did not suffer due to his lineage, the preferred tea masters of the shogun, presently irrelevant.

"I read my father's works for the first time in school, and I couldn't quite gather what all the fuss was about," Hiroshi had once said. This lukewarm reception, apparently, was due to the similarity of his writing to Takashi's. Even the brightest of higher school students would be loathe to be impressed by Hiroshi's gloomy younger brother, regardless of the quality of his writing; this applied to the shy young theatre student who obsessively read Shakespeare and Jean Racine. Later, after Hiroshi had married Ruriko, he would admit this.

"I push past a certain point, and this logic without sense is pushed into the realm of art," Takashi had written in imitation of their father. Only children, soldiers, and artists had the presence of mind to make sense of the senseless, it seemed. Similarly, in imitation of his father, it had been Takashi's habit to perch himself on a cushion alone in his room, puffing a cigarette with a sad and disharmonious expression wrenching his face, which was inscrutable. His eyes would make their way to the imitation Cézanne on the wall, or perhaps to the stack of manuscripts and books that cluttered the floor; usually situated so that an English translation of *Crime and Punishment* was positioned as a sort of capstone. In the evening, the sound of raindrops merged with the sound of the clock that echoed in the empty hallway of that Tabata house. On occasion, Takashi would mutter to himself, "Stupid!" as he shook his head from side to side, perhaps in preparation to slam his fist into the rosewood desk that had belonged to his father. These outbursts were the product of his abortive study of the maxims of François de La Rochefoucauld, the seventeenth-century soldier, writer, and nobleman. Takashi was well aware that his brothers could hear his rantings. He was certainly not the first inhabitant of this house to shout in vain… In the adjoining room, Yasushi would often be heard playing their father's wax records; their irritating cousin Yoshitoshi Kuzumaki, too, sometimes stopped by to listen to German operas, echoes of lyrics written by men long since deceased. In those days, despite the migraines, regardless of the malaise that inevitably was produced by his studies, at least Takashi had been able to write, just as fevered as his father had been during those final months. "This is what's important, for there will soon come a day when it will become unnecessary for me to write anymore. Well, that's life, isn't it?"

A year ago, Takashi had written that. How prophetic those words had been! Indeed, being correct often proved hopelessly exhausting.

"To love the art of a nation, you must know the life of a nation."

Given to similar prophetic rumination, perhaps his father had felt a similar exhaustion. Was this the vague anxiety that had led him to his death, this uncanny depth of introspection, this relentless understanding? Posthumously, his words were appropriated by figures hailing from all corners of the political spectrum. Nationalists and fascists admired his near worship of artistic purity and the glorious history of the nation; meanwhile, liberals and communists displayed keen appreciation for his opposition to militaristic aggression.

Hideo Kobayashi found the public figure of Ryūnosuke Akutagawa to be uninspiring; perhaps they were too similar in temperament, both of them being antiquarians with excessively artistic inclinations. "I had no feeling of sympathy for his suicide. I felt, rather, that his skepticism should have taken him much further. Akutagawa clung stubbornly to the intellectualism of Gourmont and Anatole France, whom he evidently loved. But I thought he should have had something more vital and intense, a higher speed intellectualism. Since that time, I have not re-read Akutagawa. Were I to read him again today, how would I react? Perhaps I would be surprised and discover in Akutagawa a traditional Japanese poet." *How glib*, Takashi thought…

Traditional Japanese poets certainly had a predilection, or perhaps predestination, for early death.

Meanwhile, Kan Kikuchi, whose diminutive presence Takashi now missed greatly in his fitful state of homesickness, had written of the man Takashi still thought of as simply Ryū-chan, "No one in the future can emulate his lofty culture, exquisite taste, and Oriental and Western learning. As an embodiment of the ancient tradition and taste of the Orient and the knowledge and taste of the Occident, he will remain a representative writer of Japan at this period of transition." Jun'ichirō Tanizaki, with whom Takashi's father had been debating during the six months leading up to his death, had simply written, "His is an agonizing soul gifted with lucid intelligence and breathtaking versatility, yet equipped with a constitution and temperament least fit to live in this world."

His son, a man who had inherited his father's gifts and failings, was presently being sent to fight in a war that he frankly didn't take much of an interest in.

"today I go to war
without looking back;
it's a humble shield
I become
for my Emperor"

— 'Man'yōshū,' as quoted by Saitō Mokichi,
physician to Ryūnosuke Akutagawa

IV

Vague Anxiety

To my sons:

1.   It should not be forgotten that life is always a battle until death.

2.   Therefore, do not forget to rely only on your own strength. Life should be for the purpose of cultivating your own strength.

3.   Ryūichi Oana is to take the place of your father. Therefore, the teachings of Oana are to be followed, including in spiritual institution and edification.

4.   If you lose the battle of your own life, then learn from your father's suicide. But, like your father, avoid harming others.

5.   Although it is difficult to know your destiny, you should strive to be self-reliant, not burden your family, and abandon your desires. This will enable you to forge a smooth path in the future.

6.   Please have mercy on your mother. Do not change your aspirations due to this mercy, but recognize it as a way for your mother to be happy in the future.

7.   You will inevitably be neurotic, like your father. Be especially careful about this.

8.   Your father loves you. (If I didn't love you, then I would still have found a way to live.)

Ryūnosuke Akutagawa,
July 23, 1927

Takashi's father had failed to commit suicide twice during perhaps the most productive year of his dazzling yet brief career; while always morbid and prone to depression, two years prior, he had firmly committed himself to death by suicide. Hanging he had ruled out, as it violated his sense of aesthetics; vain, he feared his tall, lean form becoming ugly in death. Leaping and suicide by train he had decided against for similar reasons of visual indignity. As he was a strong swimmer, drowning was not an option, for he feared his own animal instinct. He died by a fatal dose of the tranquilizer Veronal after two years filled with little beyond thoughts of death and dreams of terror. Only sorrow remained.

Ryūnosuke Akutagawa had been cursed with a morbid fear of inheriting his mother's mental illness; his writing was replete with such phrases as "hereditary insanity" and "the son of a lunatic." By all accounts, his only memories of the mother who had withered and died while he was still a child were those of a silent madness, by turn detached, polite, remarkable in her haughty docility; or terrified of the demons of air and darkness that tormented her in the guise of fox spirits. Meanwhile, Ryūnosuke's beautiful, tortured mother haunted him. He once saw her face on a stranger in the street. Increasingly vivid nightmares alongside hallucinations of translucent cogwheels that partially blocked his vision weighed heavily in this decision for voluntary death, despite his feelings of sorrow at leaving a twenty-seven-year-old widow and three fatherless sons, of whom the youngest would be left with no memories of his father, only words. This sorrow did not have the power to overthrow his desire to leave his sons free from memories of a raving madman that would no doubt contribute to their anxiety regarding their respective futures.

Takashi Akutagawa had certainly inherited the fears of his deceased father. His father, himself a skeptic of the so-called Taishō Democracy, had been witness to the rise of Japanese nationalism. As both a romantic poet in the tradition of Wordsworth or Keats and a son of the aristocracy in the vein of Saneatsu Mushanokōji, he was torn between the conflicting tides of liberal naturalism and fanatical monarchism; as though wandering through a solitary hell, he'd found a home in neither, taking solace only in death rather than drifting into the extremities of either decadence or austerity. Takashi, then, was witness to the culmination of his father's most absurd fears coming to a terrifying fruition.

"The world I am now living in is one of diseased nerves, lucid as ice. Such voluntary death must give us peace, if not happiness."

Unlike his father, Takashi had no memories of a passive lunatic who occasionally disturbed the piercing silence with a vacant shriek directed at a ceiling that descended to reach those sunken, bloodshot eyes. He only remembered a man who had once drawn him something he'd called a cigarette dragonfly, dipping a finely pointed calligraphy brush in blue black ink and using the bindings of the freshly replaced tatami mats as his ersatz canvas; Takashi and Hiroshi had laughed as their mother had scolded their father, elegant even with his bemused smile and downcast eyes. The brothers, too, had giggled as their father had drawn a kappa chasing their nagging auntie, a smirk bringing levity to his morose expression. This, too, had gotten him a scolding, even as their mother's bright eyes revealed nothing beyond good humor. Even before his conscription, Takashi's nerves had been strained by the war. His father now knew a peace so entirely foreign in this era of conflict and competing hatreds. Haunted by nightmares in his life, his premature death had spared him this present nightmare of the insanity of a tyrannical regime. Meanwhile, what could best be described as an ultranationalist hysteria weighed heavily on the shoulders of his son, soon to arrive in Japanese-occupied Korea. In an especially spiteful twist of fate, Ryūnosuke Akutagawa had written multiple pieces denouncing Japanese subjugation of Koreans, especially in the wake of the great Kantō earthquake of 1923. Takashi held no particular animosity towards Koreans; truly, he had no strong opinions regarding them one way or the other. Much like his father, he felt himself being inexorably carried towards the cruel fate that beckoned him, regardless of his own inclinations.

* * *

The house in which Takashi had been raised had been a veritable hermitage to the literary arts, a sanctuary of poetry. Each weekend, the small Tabata home would transform into a veritable literary salon; Takashi and Hiroshi would listen through the thin sliding doors as as some of the greatest artistic minds in Japan discussed matters of culture, literature, and philosophy, which eventually devolved into ravings about politics or tales of drunken, often lewd, escapades involving women, highly paid or otherwise. "Chōkōdo Shujin," the lacquered plaque above the door to their father's study read. Precocious, the two boys had fancied themselves rather worldly as they surreptitiously listened to descriptions of Kafū Nagai's "appreciation" of Russian ballerinas, resulting in their father shouting "Nagai!" with a raised fist, much to the embarrassment of a shy, young Yasunari Kawabata and the amusement of the painter Ryūichi Ōana. Regardless, their father had been awestruck by the performance of Anna Pavlova's *Dying Swan* in 1922 when she and her troupe had performed in Asakusa.

Now, Kafū Nagai had deliberately ceased writing, his own form of silent defiance, protesting the government that so crushed his spirit. Jun'ichirō Tanizaki was being criticized for his novel of the vicissitudes of the status of a family much like his own as "insufficiently patriotic." Meanwhile, Tanizaki had translated *The Tale of Genji* into modern Japanese. Instead of being surrounded by a small coterie of melancholic writers and artists, Takashi prepared to pass another dark night beneath that chilled hull of tempered steel, surrounded by men who would soon sleep easily even as they edged ever closer to conquered territory.

As he began to write a letter to Hiroshi on the conspicuously beige
army stationary, addressing it to that temporary Chōfu address, the
sun had begun to set; the wind had risen with the fall of evening, and
the hulking ship rocked especially softly for a vessel of its dimensions.
He imagined planes flying overhead as the letter reached his brother.
As though recoiling from the oppression of silence, the metal groaned.
Below, the labyrinthine system of engines and boilers seemed to
breathe, to pulse on its own accord... This ship that carried Takashi to
a place that would no doubt soon reek of death seemed frightfully
alive, itself an organism all its own. Surely his brother would laugh
at these clichéd impressions; certainly, he'd expect something more
original from the heir of a literary master. "How original, a sunset as
a metaphor for death," he'd once chided an earlier vignette, narrowing his eyes as his lips turned up in a sarcastic smile. Later, Hiroshi
had admitted that his impression of the tale was actually quite favorable. Takashi had once again fallen prey to these banalities of youth,
these blossoms of naïveté. Perhaps that was to be his fate. This prospect caused him little sorrow.

The colors of the sunset he viewed through the faint fog of the
porthole, though, were undeniably beautiful, almost floral in their
richness. It seems curious to describe blackness as purple, like a gemstone, but, indeed, it was, and yet if he were to shift his gaze upwards,
it was a deeper blue than the sea, pierced by a thin silver moon. The
sun had departed the sky, yet still its faceted aura lingered in the
gloom of the empty sea. There was something mercurial about this
transient night sky, whose previously golden clouds, curling over the
ocean, had now become invisible. Some things can truly be expressed
only in verse, as his words were powerless to capture such a grand
vision of the cosmos. This evening, he decided against committing to
paper such a description, as he presently lacked the strength, and so

he simply wrote that it was beautiful beyond description. The sunset would remain confined to the prison of his memory.

So many positions had drastically shifted in the landscape of Takashi's mind since his departure from Japan. Abstractions seemed precariously close to becoming reality; polished, his chrysanthemum-emblazoned rifle had not yet been aimed at another man, and the boots stowed in his footlocker had never once been dirtied by foreign soil. That bayonet, too, sharp as the blue moon, had never pierced human flesh. The only blood that Takashi had ever spilled had been that of his brothers, and even that had only been the result of a bloodied nose after some ridiculous fight.

"Our father was a famous artist, and yet here you are, nearly flunking out of music class!"

No different than any other brothers in Japan or elsewhere, he and Yasushi had wrestled in the small but tidy parlor, shattering a pale blue vase; Hiroshi had sighed, rolling his eyes in an exaggerated fashion before leaving the room, taking with him the bearing of haughty indifference. Takashi soon lost his fighting spirit.

"Some actor!" he'd shouted after Hiroshi, who had earlier been rehearsing his lines for a school production of *The Merchant of Venice*.

Takashi would have been thoroughly grateful if he were to only ever experience combat with his brothers, content with spilling only the blood of his kin over superficial matters. Such wounds required little effort to mend. He had not chosen to take up this rifle or to board this ship; he had not chosen the land of his birth. Even so, he would soon serve as an instrument of death, enacting the orders of those above him and inevitably causing irreparable destruction in the name of national honor. How many lives would he ruin? Many of the men he would have no choice but to kill or maim would likely be conscripts, much like himself. How many mothers would mourn the loss of their sons who could hardly be called men? Perhaps some of them were married, or had sweethearts waiting to be made brides; how many women's hearts would be broken because of this rifle so graciously given to him by the emperor? How many of them had children of their own... The first corpse Takashi had ever seen had been that of his father. Ryūichi Ōana had painted the scene. His father had looked like a pale, beautiful angel... Death had resembled sleep, and his father had appeared pale and calm once he'd deprived himself of the breath that had so tormented him. He had fallen into nothingness as he read the book of Matthew, a worn leather Bible perched atop his breast in death as a light rain fell.

"And they that passed by reviled him, wagging their heads, And saying, Thou that destroyest the temple, and buildest it in three days, save thyself. If thou be the Son of God, come down from the cross. Likewise also the chief priests mocking him, with the scribes and elders, said, He saved others; himself he cannot save."

Ryūnosuke Akutagawa had expired before having reached the resurrection of Christ. His death had been voluntary; conscripted into life, he had deserted, taking no one with him. Takashi had no such option and could now only deprive other men of their lives and their survivors of their loved ones. He was in no position to protest, for he feared the consequences to his mother and brothers; for them, he was forced to deprive strangers of those they held dear.

"It can't be helped," his father had written.

"It can't be helped," Sōseki Natsume, his father's sensei, who had died six years prior to his birth, had written. A certain character in one of his novels had gone insane; more than anything, Takashi's father had reminded Sōseki of this sensitive genius driven to madness by the intricacies of life in modern society. Civilization had torn his soul in two.

The war would be lost. "It can't be helped." Takashi said the words aloud.

From all that Takashi had read, the military superiority of the English navy combined with the sheer numbers of the American army produced the inevitability that Japan would not win this war that had begun after the bombing of an obscure harbor. This was antithetical

"Ceaseless motion, ceaseless violent deaths, ceaseless escape from cold objectivity — by now, I could no longer live without such mysteries. And — needless to say — within each mystery there lay a small imitation of death. All unawares I had embarked on a kind of pitiless round."

— Yukio Mishima,
Sun and Steel

V

The Sun Itself Had Crashed to Earth

THE BRIEF novelty of life on foreign soil lent a certain levity, a faint lightness, to the darkness and ennui that had cast its jaundiced shadow over Takashi's spirit. When an individual is the recipient of a certain amount of suffering, he risks developing a tolerance to it. Pain serves as a sort of inoculation against its aftershocks. This usurping of an unpleasant routine held off the formation of such a nonchalant attitude regarding misfortune. The disruption of this system soon defaulted to a state of perilous monotony, and Takashi continued his days as though a somnambulist, semi-conscious of the men and objects surrounding him. He'd left an island to occupy a peninsula, an extension of a continent, neither entirely isolated nor fully embraced by any sort of landscape. Now in Korea, one day dragged him with it into the haze of the next; through the sheer momentum of time, he continued on in existential tedium. Individual days became indistinguishable, their borders defining themselves by vague abstraction even as the Empire of Japan's territory expanded. This expansion without limits would no doubt lead to a violent collapse; infinite progress is an impossibility in any society, whether in the past or in the present.

Japan had replaced its ancient theology of eight million gods and demons with a macabre eschatology of frightful modernity, substituting death for impossible victory; life became nothing beyond a demonstration of patriotism stripped bare of emotion. No doubt this would be a frightening prospect for Western logic, shaking the very foundations of minds trained from childhood to value living for its own sake, regardless of the quality or dignity present in or absent from such a life.

For the first time in his life, Takashi was acutely conscious of being Japanese. On this soil, he was not only a man, but a defiantly Japanese man; quite likely, he thought, "man" was not the first word to come to mind when these civilians looked at him. To them, Takashi was no longer a man. He had ceased to be classed as the son of Ryūnosuke Akutagawa, and was similarly denied the title of poet or writer.

"Foreigner."

"Soldier."

"Fascist."

At the time of the great Kantō earthquake of 1923, Takashi had not yet reached his first year. Much of Tokyo had gone up in flames; in preparation for such a disaster, after leaving Hiroshi, Takashi, and their mother safely on the lawn, his father had run back into the house to retrieve some of his books at his wife's suggestion. He returned with the Bible, *The Communist Manifesto*, and a book of Sōseki Natsume's handwritten calligraphy. Immediately after the family of four had finished lunch, Ryūnosuke Akutagawa had poured himself a cup of green tea, which had then begun to clatter on the surface of the table. The quivering of his left hand was unrelated to the number of pills he had taken that day. The earth beneath the house had heaved violently, as though some monstrous leviathan had wrenched itself beneath the foundation; the soil writhed, and the wooden walls moaned as though they, too, feared some sort of volcanic eruption. It was as though the earth had been subject to a fit of stomach cramps. The magnitude 7.3 quake had caused no magma to spew forth from the cracked earth, and the demons of hell had not seen fit to manifest themselves. Instead, flames gnawed their way through row upon row of those boxy grey houses of paper and wood that had recently sprung up throughout Tokyo like so many cemeteries, their burnt out skeletons housing grotesquely twisted bodies.

The police department and the Kabuki-za, rebuilt after having been destroyed in an electrical fire the previous year, had burned. Sensō-ji in Asakusa had burned. Over 100,000 perished in this radical shifting of tectonic plates. The Rikugun Honjo Hifukusho had been engulfed in a tornado of flame, resulting in the immolation of some 38,000; at this army depot, civilians seeking shelter had not died in battle, but had instead perished due to an act of either nature or God. For three days, the fires had raged. The fortunate were cremated. Others were tangled much like molten drips of wax clinging to faded tapirs, their bodies taking on the qualities of dampened terra cotta. In the aftermath of this mouldering hellscape, Ryūnosuke Akutagawa had been tasked with acting as a sort of neighborhood watchman. Numerous fires sprung up in the decaying ruin. Superstitious neighbors blamed Chinese and Korean immigrants, on occasion tying them to stakes and flogging them. Takashi's father, wearing a pith helmet and carrying a slim bamboo stick, had proved to be the salvation of many foreigners in Tokyo; the local police had seen fit to deputize the writer, tall and intelligent. If nothing else, seeing that strong figure, that romantic poet cloaked in the uniform of respectability, had been beneficial for neighborhood morale. Rice and cigarettes had purchased the lives of frightened strangers.

Hallucination, indoctrination… One was the product of internal disharmony; the other was caused by external force, even if unbeknownst to the recipient. One harmed only the self. Both seemed kinder than this cruel awareness of sanity, this silent observation of discord.

Presently, the local Koreans saw this visiting man who was now called Sergeant Takashi Akutagawa as no such hero. Here, the lunatic's son could not barter cigarettes and rice for dignity. Rather than a defender, this polite young man was seen as an occupier, an interloper;

to their eyes, his very presence was invasive, regardless of either his lack of colonial intention or his quiet political disinterest. He lacked the freedom to be respectably disengaged.

When Japan had bombed the Americans, getting into this ridiculous war that was now being waged on multiple continents, Takashi had initially dismissed it as a brief moment of national insanity. Most of those around him had assumed the war would be either won or lost in a matter of mere months, a trifling affair. The eccentric collection of writers and artists who had continued to bolster the remnants of the Akutagawa family after the death of its patriarch had largely denounced the war. "This is absurd; it's all just too stupid," any number of them would say. "There's no way it will last." On occasion, a drunken shout of "Banzai!" would resound in mockery of the regime, resulting in the laughter of those three fatherless boys and the diminutive widow who had conspicuously decided against remarriage, choosing to love no one else.

Certainly, the war was absurd, but absurdity has its own sort of cunning longevity. Stupidity allows for the continuation of precious few pleasant accumulations; destruction, then, stupidity has a frightfully acute knack for prolonging. Modern man lacks the introspection to realize this until the damage has progressed past the point of becoming irreparable, having grown malignant and metastasizing. In December of 1941, the sixteenth year of Shōwa, Japan had bombed America; in December of 1943, the eighteenth year of Shōwa, Takashi, as a member of the Imperial 22nd Army Korean Corps, participated in the occupation that he had come to find morally repugnant. The winds chilled him.

"Great nations don't collapse," Jun'ichirō Tanizaki had said, referring to China, whose borders Japan had also breached. "Of course we'll lose." He'd boasted of never having voted, a smile crossing that familiar round face. He had then argued with some of the other writers about the Man'yōshū, an eighth-century anthology of poetry, criticizing it as a relic of senseless emperor worship and instead championing the superior logic of the Kokinshū and the deftly navigated poetic circumlocutions of the Shinkokinshū. Takashi, meanwhile, preferred Paul Verlaine and François de La Rochefoucauld, shyly demonstrating his superior French that he was soon to make copious use of as an army translator. He detected a certain sadness in the eyes of that great statesman of Japanese literature, becoming all too aware of the similarities inextricably entwining him with his doomed father.

* * *

Until he'd received his call-up paper, mailed for the price of one sen and five rin, Takashi had considered himself to be sovereign over the course of his destiny, even when taking into consideration the morbid likelihood of his having inherited his father's disease; for the first time, he was exposed to the negation of his individualism resulting in a complete deprivation of freedom. Even supposing that seishin-bun-retsu-byo, very literally "split mind disease," had been passed down, it would not have curtailed Takashi's art. What artist ever produced his greatest works in a state of contentment? A laughable prospect. Van Gogh, that pipe-smoking victim of psychological gloom who painted emerald and gold cypress roots beneath the blinding sun of the French Riviera, would have seen none of his fatal beauty were it not for his disease. The last year of his father's life, too, that year of torturous disintegration of the self, had resulted in some of his most striking masterpieces. His splintered visions were surely resplendent, even when reducing that gentle soul to terror. Valiantly, he'd persisted in the documentation of his own demise.

"I am living now in the unhappiest happiness imaginable. Yet, strangely, I have no regrets. I just feel sorry for anyone unfortunate enough to have had a bad husband, a bad son, a bad father like me."

Takashi did not remember a bad father, and his mother, Fumi, had no memories of a bad husband. She'd loved her husband even after his death; no man could have taken the vacant place of Japan's great romantic in her wounded heart. Meanwhile, as much as Takashi loved those writers and artists who served as surrogate fathers, or perhaps uncles, the genuine article was irreplaceable, sovereign. Certainly, Ryūnosuke had had his vices, namely barbiturates and women, and yet those were far from the first things that came to mind when his few memories of his father surfaced. Takashi remembered his father's eyes; those beautiful, clear eyes that reflected nothing but love when they fell upon his wife and children. The brilliance behind them was undeniable, unshakable even in his state of exacerbated frailty. Firmly showing conviction yet easily frightened, those eyes, too, readily served as mirrors reflecting inwardly on a fearful, delicate soul. An elegant man of a thoroughly dignified bearing, this duality presented itself to startling effect. His father had been a remarkable man, by all accounts. His failings had only served to magnify this.

"Le beau est toujours bizarre;" "The beautiful is always bizarre," Baudelaire had written. Takashi's father had truly believed that all of life was not worth a single line of Baudelaire. A man of unabashed conviction, he had lived and died by those words that gave something that could not quite be described as "meaning" to his life. Indeed, the autobiography that could be described as half prose, half poetry had been published posthumously. "Beauty is always bizarre. I do not mean to say that it is deliberately, coldly bizarre, for in that case it would be a monster that has escaped from the confines of existence. I mean that it always contains a certain amount of strangeness, naïve strangeness, unforced and even unconscious, and that it is this strangeness that stamps it as beautiful." Baudelaire presently rested beneath the mossy soil of the Cimetière du Montparnasse. Lichen the color of poison had surely begun climbing that austere headstone. Much as his father had, Takashi wished to make a pilgrimage to that grave; presently, France was as free as Korea, occupied by that Vichy regime headed by Philippe Pétain. Beyond that, Takashi was ignorant of world events, forbidden by his platoon leader from reading his beloved French literary periodicals. The magazine *Le Temps* had been banned the previous year, regardless.

The present atmosphere was nothing if not discouraging. Those who had been given the reins to the destiny of Japan had remained willfully ignorant of the turmoil assailing the hearts and minds of much of its populace. Anguish and ambivalence vied for superiority, resulting in a sort of passive despondency. This war would certainly result in the downfall and subsequent rebirth of that spiritually terrorized populace that Takashi had physically abandoned for the shores of this tawny soil marked by both soaring mountains and vast coastal plains.

The destructive logic of the creation of history continued. Takashi knew no more freedom than these Koreans; his mind, too, was oppressed. The cruelest form of imprisonment was the incarceration of the mind, the impossibility of any form of escape from the self. Here, in this occupied territory, Takashi understood the torment that had resulted in his father's death. *Were justice and freedom mutually exclusive?* he wondered. Could this fractured world be rebuilt? Those sturdy of constitution were physically destroyed in combat; those fragile of mind were either discarded or forced to face solitary ruin.

* * *

In school, like most children, Takashi had learned a poem by the famed General Maresuke Nogi, that reluctant hero of Port Arthur, "Outside the Fortress at Goldland." The Chinese-inspired verse had been composed following the death of Nogi's second son, Yasusuke.

> Hills, river, grass, trees,
> Truly desolate, a ten mile stretch.
> A foul, blood-soaked wind
> Over a fresh battlefield.
> The horses do not stir,
> The men do not speak.
> In the slanted rays of the setting sun,
> Outside the Fortress at Goldland.

Ryūnosuke Akutagawa had evidently felt no small amount of sympathy for the Nogi sons, having written about them in his journals. Indeed, his short story "The General" had been written the year of Takashi's birth.

Yasusuke Nogi had been assumed by most to be the favored son of his famously upright father. At the time of his death, he had been carrying dispatches from the front lines of that critical position at 203 Meter Hill when a Russian bullet had struck him. He died on impact. Unlike his first son, Katsusuke, whose name meant "son of victory," Nogi had been present to claim Yasusuke's body. The round had pierced the back of his beloved son's skull.

"Was it after he had completed his task, or was it before?" the general had asked, his soft voice low and melodic.

The staff officer replied that Yasusuke had delivered the documents bravely even while under heavy artillery fire; the entire scene illuminated by flashing grenades, he'd been killed while returning to his regiment. Nogi gazed vacantly out the window of the makeshift field hospital before nodding, displaying a deceptively calm façade. "I often wondered how I would apologize to His Majesty and to the people for having killed so many of my men. But now that my son has been killed…"

Shirai, the staff officer, reported that General Nogi silently wept before saying, "Cremate it, turn it to ashes." His son now reduced to "it," Nogi then turned his eyes to the window, perhaps so that his face might remain unseen in his moment of sorrow.

On those petrol-colored Manchurian wastelands, the bodies of both Japanese and Russians were left to decay where they had fallen, taking on the unearthly colors of the soil that was foreign to men of both sides. Yasusuke was an exception; posthumously, that young man whose name loosely translated to "son of peace" received a promotion to first lieutenant, and his ashes were sent home to Japan, to the Countess Nogi, who would never be a widow.

"Ours was a spirit of selflessness between master and servant bound by the principle of obligation transcending obligation; in which looking at death came to be like being reduced to death. In this way death was not made light of, but deeply revered as death in its truest sense. In other words, through death, life was perfected."

— *The Essence of the National Polity*

V I

I Write in the Ash

CLOUDS like rose-colored plumes of smoke illuminated a sky the shade of Himalayan rock salt, translucent in the dusk. The effect of the chilled air against such warmly illuminated scenery was uncanny, but that did little to detract from its beauty; somehow, the sunset had taken on the quality of frost, and yet there was little moisture in the quiet air of early spring. The Korean peninsula should have been silent at this hour, and yet sounds of human life abounded. In the cold evening, the wind quickly swept this meaningless sound into the Yellow Sea, which sparkled as a faint glimpse of the sun, golden and resplendent, disappeared beneath those frigid topaz waters.

It was a mundane Friday, and the air smelled of mountain foliage, polished leather, and an unidentifiable dustiness that suggested machinery. Even in the night air, the perspiration of both man and beast could be detected; the scent of manure lent an earthiness to the aroma that would have otherwise carried the heady air of cologne. Takashi assumed his brother, Hiroshi, was having a curry, as the Imperial Japanese Navy had evidently adopted that practice of the Royal Navy in order to aid sailors in maintaining some semblance of timekeeping on those endless foreign seas; with such a practice, dates could maintain relevance even against the shifting tides of dissolution. Upon reading his brother's letters, Takashi could not help but be amused by this: the only bodies of water surrounding

Chōfu were the Tama and Iruma rivers. Saneatsu Mushanokōji, one of their father's favorite novelists and presently a playwright, hailed from Chōfu; Takashi could not help but wonder if Hiroshi received visits from the famed writer much loved by both of them. Before his conscription, Hiroshi had acted in one of Mushanokōji's plays to much acclaim, and their politics were in alignment, both of them being more conservative than either Takashi or Ryūnosuke and yet still party to their admiration. Takashi had not bothered to see his brother's performance. As a child, he recalled Hiroshi playing the part of a shepherd in a school Christmas pageant. He recalled the light in his brother's eyes when, after the performance, Hiroshi had spotted their father waiting in the wings to congratulate his oldest son, oblivious to the housewives whose eyes were drawn to the tall, handsome writer. Presently, that brother he idolized was praying over planes that would carry young men to youthful death.

Meanwhile, Takashi's dinner had consisted of a single serving of steamed rice with tinned tuna and a pickled plum. Saké and a copious amount of cigarettes staved off hunger; already, he'd begun to lose weight. Much like his father, in times of stress, this happened, and his cheeks had begun to take on a hollowness beyond his years. In the mirror, he saw his father's large, frightened eyes, clear even in the burning darkness. The face of a deceased pacifist in a military uniform: his own appearance unsettled him, and yet he was incapable of articulating this poorly formed fear of the self that suffused each day with a routine sense of dread.

* * *

"Japanese Bridges" was one of the few things he was allowed to read.

"In Oriental culture, there was a blossoming and a withering away of isolation and no age of discovery by the masses; such an age does not even exist anywhere in our history. The birth of the contradictions of modernity in our country Japan — which became a modern state having skipped over a cultural renaissance — forced us to graft ourselves onto the European spirit, which emerged from the Renaissance neglecting its own lineage of medieval culture. The sense of impermanence — born from being haunted by the spirit of the evil specter of that ancient Asian invasion — strangely coursed through the actions of the masses and was the same spirit as that behind the practice of praying for Amitahba's appearance to come at the moment of one's death. Even the invasion itself was not a conquest or artifice but nature itself."

Now surrounded by those who slept easily beneath the darkened evening sky, above him a roof of corrugated aluminum, so dissimilar from the harmoniously constructed edifices with thatched roofs inhabited by the locals, Takashi could do nothing but think, passing the silence until those demure rays of dawn pierced the blackened steel windowpanes. Somehow, the sharply arched wooden roofs of those houses in Tabata floated in his mind as freely as the flotsam swirling in those waters of the Sumida River, somehow both pure and polluted, but recalled with remarkable clarity. The shores of Japan were bitterly distant.

"Sway with the current, and avoid persecution," his capricious thoughts told him. "Fate ordains your heart to wither in the darkness," and so his spirit weakened as if in divine accordance.

Among the others, those who slept so comfortably and whose faint breathing presently brought Takashi to the brink of anger as he could no longer direct his concentration towards nothingness... Their unpracticed minds had grown accustomed to these tenuously stable tides, those pale blue waves of thoughtless "sense." Yes, they'd grown accustomed to the currents of the times. The waves thrashed against reason itself, and yet they took no time to question such irrational devotion. They subsisted in a state of pampered blindness. Beyond this, they did not give a damn. The retreating waves remained unquestioned. Certainly, no one wondered why these men were so cruelly, callously exposed to such torments of water and time. Even if it had occured to them to question their status, they remained powerless to improve their situation. "Sway day and night," and so they sway, complicit and content.

According to fate, they should grow in the darkness, and so they thrived. Darkness beckoned their mechanical dance with thunderous drums, and so onward they marched.

How many men had Yojūro Yasuda seduced with the beauty of his lyrical composition, that siren song bemoaning a loss of purity, a dilution of the unfettered heroic spirit present in the heart of every Japanese man from ancient times? Even Takashi, indeed a vehement pacifist in the tradition of his father, could not deny the loveliness of these words, even as he decried them. With this loveliness, though, came a sort of power that verged on the sacred; with these words, so elegantly wrought in the tradition of Ariwara no Narihira, that Heian poet rumored to be the father of the Emperor Yōzei, an unspeakable strength quietly asserted itself. How many men had fallen beneath the sway of romantic language and been lured by verse to face violent death on foreign soil? The lyricism of rage… Propaganda, too, could take on the form of poetry.

"Just as Bashō said that what penetrates all things is one and the same, theirs was a faith in a lineage of the past, present, and future serving in the defense of beauty."

And who would not want to serve as a defender of beauty, to acknowledge the value of noble lineage? Even his father had written, "The people are quiet conservatives. Institutions, ideas, the arts, religion — all of these, to be loved by the people, must be clad in the colors of previous eras." Twenty years later, the passage following that particular aphorism was censored: "Men of antiquity taught that making the people stupid was the Tao of governing the country. Work either to make them as much stupider as possible — or, by whatever means, as much wiser."

After his conscription, Takashi's romantic aestheticism had been shattered, demolished as his innermost sense of ethics asserted itself, casting a vague sense of guilt around the poetry he wrote to to his brother and mother back home in Tokyo. In verse, he carefully veiled any thoughts on desertion. They made no mention of this in any of their replies, and so he wondered if his intent had eluded them, his writing being perhaps too vague. Still, his principles, that fastidious upright sense of morality he had inherited, prevented him from acting on such ethical assertions. In short, he was too polite to practice his individualism. His reserves defeated, sleep consumed him shortly before the dawn, leaving him with little time to experience something that was more of a fragmented memory than a dream. The past sheltered him from the interminable present.

At the time, there had been five of them. Yasushi was still a baby, and so his mother had decided ιo leave him with Aunt Fuku while the rest of the family traveled outside the city to visit her mother and sister. Her husband's failing health was her primary concern. In that second-class train car on the Tōkaidō line, Ryū-chan, dressed in a heavily starched kimono, had finished reading the stack of books he'd brought with him; silently, he'd taken the book that had been perched on Jun'ichirō Tanizaki's knee and begun reading it. Takashi and Hiroshi had giggled, and "Uncle" Tanizaki, famously fearful of trains, soon appeared visibly calmer than their father, who finished the novel with frightful speed. Its language, author, and title were irrelevant. Ryūnosuke Akutagawa, christened the Demon of Letters by both the press and his sons, flaunted his talent without reserve even during that year of his greatest weakness. Then seated on Tanizaki's knee, Takashi had resolved to one day match this poetic fury.

Once having arrived at that two-story house in the pleasantly chilled air near Tokyo Bay, the young boys had passed the time in idyllic leisure, climbing trees and chasing the white leghorn chickens, so exotic, whose eggs were the color of polished rocks at the base of a shallow river bed. Their father painted them in oil. These eggs provided their breakfast, far nicer than the eggs in Tokyo, Tanizaki proclaimed, and still Ryū-chan was often too unwell to eat.

"Can't you see he's suffering?"

Petite and gentle, her soft voice abruptly sharp, Takashi's mother had chastised her brother-in-law, a corpulent man who had a nasty temper and a habit of taunting her excessively lean husband whenever the opportunity presented itself. The young boy could not say why, but something about that moment felt "adult," and he felt his cheeks prickle with warmth as he saw the hurt in his father's eyes transformed into something victorious. This was quickly forgotten when his father broke the silence with a rare smile, charming even in his pain.

"You two, why don't you play on the lawn?"

Their fat uncle glowered as Takashi and Hiroshi ran outside into the salted air, the hems of their brightly colored kimonos fluttering in the breeze. Their father, too, stood, and silently began one of his characteristically long walks, a book tucked beneath his arm and a straw hat shading his bloodless complexion from the sun of noon. When he returned, the sun had begun to set. Even in the country, electrical power lines cast their unnatural shadows onto the dusty lanes. His sunken eyes, still clear as ever, were wild, as though he'd seen something unspeakable. He remained silent, hanging his hat on a stand by the door after removing his geta. Until he spoke, the air was only broken by the rustling of that starched grey kimono, which made his skin appear even whiter. He looked like a ghost, Takashi thought, and yet he felt no fear of this man who had been reduced to the colors of ash and wind.

"I'm going upstairs to lie down," his father said, his voice deep yet soft. Weariness seemed to weigh heavily upon him. The sound did not carry far beyond the two boys, who had earlier abandoned their tree climbing in favor of tossing a ball sewn from red and burgundy chintz precariously near the picture windows overlooking the ocean. The ball fell to the floor as their father ascended the stairs.

"He's having one of his migraines," Hiroshi said with the haughty assurance of one who had known their father for two years longer than his kid brother. From upstairs, the moans of one in pain could be heard.

Like the crashing of glass, the sound of a bugle awoke Takashi before the first light of dawn advanced upon the mountain peaks surrounding the encampment in Seoul.

"Down in our hearts we cried and cursed this government
every time when we showered with sand. We slept in
the dust; we breathed the dust; we ate the dust."

— Joseph Kurihara,
internee at Manzanar internment camp

VII

I Shall Be Nothing, the Wind, the Sky

THE YONGSAN DISTRICT, located in central Seoul, is situated along the northern bank of the Han River. According to legend, Yongsan, which translates as "Dragon Mountain," is so named because of the peculiar shape of the nearby mountains, which the locals describe as resembling a dragon. Takashi saw no such form in the iron-colored peaks looming in the distance like distant cannons. Meanwhile, the oldest recorded reference to Yongsan occurs in a myth involving the appearance of two dragons over Hangang River during the Nambuyeo Dynasty. Beyond this, the lore surrounding the name of this Dragon Mountain becomes rather ambiguous, much like the tales of Ise.

Ryūnosuke Akutagawa had written a similar story, although centered around a lake in Japan rather than a mountain in Korea; famously born during the year of the dragon, the month of the dragon, and even the very hour of the dragon, his name translated as "son of the dragon." He had always disliked this, finding it sentimental, and presently, Takashi could not help but wonder if there were, indeed, no coincidences in this inconvenient thing called life. His father would have found such thoughts ridiculous, no doubt, in spite of his superstitious nature, and would have seen fit to make some sarcastic remark to his poetically inclined second son.

"In the realm of art there is no such thing as pause. 'No progress' means regress. When an artist regresses, there always begins a sort of automatism; that is, he turns out the same sort of stuff. Once this automatism sets in, the artist is clearly on the verge of death. When I wrote 'The Dragon' I faced such an artistic death."

On the verge of death, indeed.

Beginning in 1910, Meiji 43, the Japanese had begun using Yongsan as a military base; the level ground in the western area of the district was especially useful for rail transport. In the north and the east, the terrain grows steeper until reaching its peak at the granite cliffs of Nansam, resulting in flooding during the rainy season. This proved inconvenient to the Japanese troops stationed there, but they managed with little difficulty, their spirits as yet unbroken, having not yet seen combat.

"I have not yet killed a man," Takashi thought; what a strange idea to occupy one's mind. "Yet." An inevitability... Some things can't be helped.

Flowering cryptomeria with blossoms like paper streamers were draped over the ash-colored embankments, their crimson petals the very image of flowing streams of blood. The sharply inclined rocks of grey, meanwhile, resembled a frozen waterfall beside those petals that swayed in the perfumed breeze, so vital and alive. Beneath this was a filthy trench, its waters the dusky color of chartreuse rot. In the spring morning, the mountain veiled by mist, a multitude of prayers could be heard. All manner of Japanese accents harmonized; on foreign soil, the difference between the shrill speech of Osaka or muted Kyoto elocution became irrelevant. Kantō became indistinguishable from Kansai. Takashi, the erudite literary prodigy epitomizing old Tokyo, became yet another son of Yamato on this foreign soil, a brother, something beyond that son of the dragon writer. As the weeks became months, his status as an outsider, a maddening liability, grew increasingly distant. Prayers rose with the sun that bathed the surrounding cliffs in gold. Sakura season arrived in Seoul much as it did in Tokyo, or deep within Japan's heart of old Kyoto, although for the men of the 49ᵗʰ Infantry Division it seemed to arrive with a sort of artificial delay, as though the blossoms themselves were hesitant to make their appearance in this occupied territory; the petals drifting so gently down the Han River seemed purified by the crystalline waters. It seemed incongruous that no Shinto shrines were present on the banks surrounding those waters that reflected the sky soaring above them in the light of dawn. In Tokyo, Ueno Park in the Taitō district was renowned for its cherry blossoms; in Seoul, apparently the grounds of the Changdeokgung Palace in the Jongno district served a similar function.

Prayers in the mother tongue brought some measure of comfort to those of disparate faiths; Buddhist or Shintoist, Christians, too, all of these words harmonized within the unity of a common language. Takashi's father had been a Christian, despite his repeated denial of his own faith. Takashi had no confidence in his own vaguely defined faith. Certainly, he'd gone to Christian school, as his father had seen it a necessity that his sons learn English and Greek. Ryūnosuke Akutagawa spoke French for his art, privately translating Voltaire and Baudelaire for his own pleasure; Sergeant Takashi Akutagawa spoke French for his mother country, for pure utility.

The 49ᵗʰ Division, whose call sign was Okami 1872, or Wolf 1872, was formed on January 6, 1944 in Yongsan. Lieutenant General Saburo Takehara, a small, elegant man with a tidy moustache, served as the commander of this division formed from the remnants of the 64ᵗʰ Infantry Brigade and the 20ᵗʰ Infantry Division. The headquarters was initially located in Nara, with some of the soldiers being Korean locals, many of them having volunteered. Regardless of their places of birth, all were stationed in this place called Yongsan.

Beginning in 1887, Meiji 20, French, Chinese, and Japanese missionaries had brought their disparate incarnations of Christianity to what would soon become a bustling commercial district. No one had told him as much, but Takashi assumed he'd been sent here for this reason; otherwise, a French interpreter in Korea made little sense. He was also authorized as an interpreter for English and German, although these would likely be of little use. Recently, he had begun a study of Burmese. "The French Officer," the men of Okami now called Sergeant Takashi Akutagawa. These days, if he were to be slapped across the face, it was only in jest, and the sounds of the collision of flesh would be followed by laughter. Impeccably polished in both manner and appearance, the stylish monicker suited this docile young sergeant. He had wholly ceased to be a liability in their eyes. Instead, this pale student draftee, tall and yet of delicate constitution, had proved himself to be indispensable.

Engines could be heard in the distance. These rumblings, low as the growls of beasts and steady as the thrumming of a human pulse, presented no threat. The mechanical echoes that stirred the sky, propelling man to the heavens, were now familiar to the men of Okami 1872; these particular reverberations were now easily recognizable to them as those of Hayabusa engines, rather than enemy planes, and so these sounds of pulsing metal caused no one any degree of fear. It's startling, the degree to which mankind can acclimate itself to inhuman conditions. It seemed incongruous that no sounds of artillery rounds disturbed the bland, static quality of the air. The quiet was eerie, the Hayabusa engines no less familiar to the soldiers than the sounds of the buzzing of electric lightbulbs. Illumination could certainly be horrifying.

* * *

Hisa (Nishikawa) Kuzumaki

Kakuda-mura, Yubari-gun, Hokkaido

Thank you for your patience, Auntie. How are you? I've been working diligently every day since I joined the army, and I'm sorry I couldn't send you a letter earlier. Now, after the New Year has been replaced with the season of sakura, I'm grateful for this opportunity to once again take up a brush and practice my calligraphy, so please accept this postcard. How do you like it? You may have been worried about my departure for Korea, but please be assured that I have been in fair health since joining the army. The cold is different from that of Tokyo, but the sky above me remains changeless. The daily exercise is intense, but my heart remains strong. My body is perhaps too thin compared to my comrades, these new brothers of mine, but I will do my best to make useful the ration of energy given to me by Kami-sama. To my utmost limits, I will continue with this energy, this internalized demonstration of strength.

I don't know specific details of the conditions in Tokyo, but I do think everyone in the family is fine and safe at present.

I certainly fear I have inherited my father's weakness, but I imagine he passed on to me a measure of his strength as well. Who can say if I am unbalanced, my heart poorly calibrated? My soul is my own.

From here on, the climate will be colder; perhaps my life, should I return to the home front, will be difficult, so l will do my best to take care of myself and perhaps return to you in good spirits someday.

Korea's (Censored), Satō Unit

(Censored)

Takashi Akutagawa

* * *

Sergeant Takashi Akutagawa had been afflicted with premonitions of his own death since his bout with pleurisy before his conscription; at the time, the bones of his chest had ached as though set aflame. There was nothing to be done as chest pains led to cruel spasms. The illness had left him only after forcibly halting his studies of French for a year before his conscription, but this had no bearing on his comprehension of the language of Voltaire. His translations of the poetry of Théophile Gautier were comparable to those of Isoo Saitō, masterful by any account. His translations of Wordsworth, too, were sensitively wrought.

"Such sights, or worse, as are before me here. — Not without hope we suffer and we mourn."

This was no place for poetry. Though he presently had few opportunities, even in Yongsan, he composed modernist verse. His brother, the actor who wanted more than anything to play Hamlet, inspired some of his poems on this soil as foreign as that of Denmark.

> When you die
> The act, quiet and easy
> Close the door
> Pull the curtain
> Destroy the light

Takashi found himself on a path of discrete resignation, unable to turn back. Calmly, he sensed his own body and life soon coming to an end. Those earlier premonitions of death had begun to gain a more corporeal essence, establishing a fearsome traction. Even when presented with this, he felt no fear. Indeed, the dark levity itself girded him. What could the implicit understanding of one's own death bring if not peace? At least at the moment, his fate did not frighten him. Blessed or cursed with the sense that he was gradually becoming a prisoner to his own morose feelings, Takashi carried on, writing home in lonesome monotony. He found himself caught in the hands of the demons of war, and extricating himself had now become an impossibility.

Pleurisy had caused him to cough up blood. His brother, who had known Olivia de Havilland and Joan Fontaine, had instructed him in faking tuberculosis. Perhaps Takashi's acting skills were poor, or perhaps fate simply despised the Akutagawa family, heaping misplaced scorn upon these four survivors.

"Gentlemen! What power you have I cannot know. Neither can you yourself know. Our posterity alone can decide the question. Not until you have marched along the road to your ideals as far as you can and have dropped dead in your tracks, only at that moment can you learn the extent of your own power. You must be content to live in the works you will have accomplished. It is frivolous to try to go down in history on the merit of your name."

— Sōseki Natsume,
Nowaki

VIII

The Blame He Laid on Life

THE ROAD to Burma was built by the dead.

In a state of naturalistic desolation, the corpses did not so much give the appearance of retreating from the ground as having become the ground, itself. Marching downhill nearing a wide floodplain the color of dampened terra cotta, Takashi came to understand his father's visions of hell. He was party to a panoramic vision of the putrid banality of destruction. Beyond him were bodies, some of which could scarcely be called mere portions of bodies, flattened much like shards of pottery, the contours of their decayed flesh imprinted upon the very surface of the earth as though lending substance to it. Several of the men surrounding him gasped; the sounds of coughing gave way to the sounds of wretching. The scents were intolerable. Even so, the men continued this march towards a field of annihilation. Several times in this descent, Takashi had nearly trod upon what had initially appeared to be a rock in order to steady himself; on occasion, these "rocks" were visible as the skulls of deceased soldiers, their bodies and uniforms having decayed beyond the recognition of race or nation. At a certain point, he had very nearly planted his foot on what had appeared to be a dry patch surrounded by squelching mud. He recoiled as his eyes began to follow an indistinct outline that he soon came to recognize as the form of a man, flayed skin discolored by decay and sunlight much like tanned leather. Evidently, the soldier had been hit

and embarrassment when he realized that his father's prediction had been proved correct: China had sold her wares to the Americans for a pittance, and in doing so had purchased their loyalty. And if this behemoth was to invade Japan, or to send great numbers of men to fight on this vast and seemingly endless road paved by death... His father had not been insane.

An offensive beginning in Yunnan, led by Chinese forces commanded by General Wèi Lìhuáng, had begun to move southward. American troops under the command of General Joseph W. Stilwell, called "Vinegar Joe," according to snatches of radio broadcasts the men of Okami had been able to hear, was a former military attaché at the US legation in Beijing; they would soon link up with the Nationalist Chinese forces. These two superpowers representative of both East and West had begun to stage an invasion of northern Burma, girded by the English, from what little the poorly equipped men could gather. The Americans were evidently training Chinese army divisions to be employed against the Japanese.

All of this information was of little use for Takashi and the other men of Okami 1872, who continued their advance along the Burma road. "Heaven is Java; hell is Burma; but no one returns alive from New Guinea," or so the saying went among the enlisted men. Hell, then, was where they found themselves stationed, although things could certainly have been worse. Rumors of cannibalism among Japanese troops in New Guinea and the Philippines abounded; at least the situation in Burma did not yet seem so dire. It certainly seemed poised to eventually reach such a point, although no one dared speak of this, instead displaying a false buoyancy as they performed labor better suited to the oxen that fell over the sharply inclined cliffs of Burma with alarming regularity. No more oxen were present, some of them having been used for food.

The Burmese locals encountered by these men, dressed in threadbare uniforms and pulling carts over terrain that could be best compared to the pockmarked surface of an asteroid, were nothing if not lovely. Some of the locals resented British rule; others resented the Japanese occupying forces. Most of them simply didn't take much interest in these political matters that hardly impacted their daily lives. Takashi had begun to make himself known among the local Burmese farmers. His compatriots called him the French Officer, and these weakened but plucky conscripts who had begun to take a liking to the quiet, polite sergeant had thus convinced the Burmese to call him "Akutagawa Sensei," much to his bemusement. His mind the equal to his father's, he'd taught himself the language from an army handbook and conversations with local farmers. By any account, Takashi was fluent. The locals found him charming, and he was all too happy to share his meager rations with them, especially the children; having grown up fatherless, this proved natural to him. Old men in these rural villages situated along jade hillsides, too, appreciated idle chats with this foreign man who shared his cigarettes with them as he continued to advance alongside these units with foreign names. Briefly, they had once again become men, rather than soldiers. "Sensei" replaced "Sergeant," in Takashi's case.

* * *

Burma is a land of pagodas. Golden stupas rise from mist-laden soil; the low brush that surrounds them is revealed to be the palest of greens in the dawn, and phosphorescent dew shimmers beneath a rising sun the color of polished bronze. The pagodas outshine this newly revealed daylight. Beyond them, mountains rise in shades reminiscent of diluted black ink, faded to the color of shadow, ghostly in the distance. The landscape of this ancient land resembles an ukiyo-e print, all at once evanescent and primordial. The golden pagodas provide a bridge between these two disparate spheres.

Even in the sumptuous beauty of this sea of foliage and pagodas, memories of the march along that highway of bones were not easily lost. Anything would have been preferable to that expanse of decay occasionally interrupted by bleached bones, which sometimes resembled the white crest of a wave, a perversion of Hiroshige's famous painting. Now, in the stark daylight, the pagodas had been revealed to be not gold, but crumbling stone, grandiose even, or perhaps especially, in their ruin. It was unimaginable, the improvement in scenery. The Burmese plain was vast, apparently deserted, the stupas like the spires of cathedrals interspersed between stalks of tall, ripening bamboo that stretched until the expanse of green and grey was broken by mountains the color of faintly purple smoke, of incense. Neyraudia reynaudiana, Burmese cane, flourished beneath the sheltering shadows. Through this scenery, the road continued, having earlier been thoroughly cleared by sappers with little else to do. At last, the air was fairly clean, although booming artillery could still be heard beyond the mountains that threatened to pierce the sky. Here, there was daylight, and clouds mercifully blocked the sunlight that assailed the eyes of these weary men who did not yet fear that monotonous clamor of shelling.

Listless, his hand raised to shelter his forehead from the sun, Takashi forced himself to glance first to his left, then to his right. At certain points, the stalks of cane were as tall as the men, and equally lean. Once again, the rifle strapped to his back felt heavy; the pack containing potatoes supplied by kind Burmese farmers and a painfully diminished supply of rice, too, only furthered his exhaustion beneath their weight. He'd become accustomed to eating the rice without boiling it. Perhaps this was better, as it more easily expanded to fill his empty stomach. The man who had been marching for weeks on end may as well have been a different man from the one who had stood on the proud deck of the *Yamato* that morning in late November, the 28th, bashful and yet angered by his circumstances. By this point, he would have long since forgotten the date had it not been for the fact that it had been the last time he'd seen his mother and Yasushi. His mother had shown too much dignity to cry... He, too, took comfort in recalling that it was the 22nd that he'd last seen Hiroshi. Dates were only relevant as far as the past was concerned, for the present was interminable. Takashi could not know whether his brother was alive, or if he had joined their father in young death. These memories and uncertainties combined with the painful, unpleasant shadows of the present. The disparate spheres were wholly distinct in his mind, although this separation was only by a hair's breadth. It was a different man who was marching through this vast cemetery in the direction of smoke and thunder.

The men around Takashi appeared similarly changed, their countenances irrevocably altered; their complexions in turn sallow and jaundiced, their skin had been turned beige by the sun, as though stained by tea leaves in an inauspicious formation. The infantrymen seemed to merge with the pockmarked earth on which they trod, some of them in boots, some in woven straw sandals resembling Japanese house slippers that had been proffered by locals who'd taken a liking to these men young enough to be their sons. Takashi had delighted in practicing his Burmese with the village children, on occasion presenting them with poems written in Japanese by "Akutagawa Sensei." His oldest niece had now reached their age, four or five; Takashi could not help but wonder if Hiroshi and Ruriko had decided to have children so early in their marriage because Hiroshi's survival was increasingly perilous. Their daughter, Eiko, had already perished.

The echoes of artillery that filled the valley once again called to mind a great earthquake, although the earth had no intention of swallowing them up; doubtless, some of them wished it would be so kind. How many miles before this route was to end, or even to change? He longed for the soil of his homeland. Yes, certainly, the palest lavender plum blossoms would be sprouting from the tree on that two-story house in Tabata. The branches of the trees in his schoolyard so near the Yasukuni Shrine, too, would presently be blooming, the soft wind carrying individual petals to the moss-covered stones beneath.

Takashi's concentration on those far-off visions of beauty was shattered when a wheel of the gun carriage in front of him struck a stone, producing a loud cracking sound; by now, he was accustomed to this, and the wheel showed no sign of breaking completely. There were to be no stops for repairs, or for breath. In exhaustion, he nearly collided with the cart in front of him.

Last week, it had rained. The ground had taken on the quality of damp plaster, and four men had been needed to push a single cart, the mud reaching halfway up their calves with each labored step. Even the men who were barefoot had appeared to be wearing leather boots polished to high shine. For over ten miles, they had continued in such a manner. Somehow, this mud seemed different than that of Japan, with its tidy bronze color resembling varnished ceramic beside pale blue waters whose stillness was only interrupted by water lilies. Stretching on, the same road that had previously been congealing mire had dried into a wavelike pattern resembling the waters of a filthy canal. The gun carriages were pulled forward like ships careening over an angry sea, peaking and crashing, their sails rendered useless by the cold logic of nature.

Takashi felt weak, and yet he persisted. His breathing was labored. He took no notice of the similarly raspy breathing of those around him; their breath was indistinct from the wind that rustled the stalks of cane and deep green leaves of bamboo. Every mile or so, the shadow of a pagoda fell over the road, overlapping the shadows of bamboo that swayed so gently beneath the sun. The canteen strapped to his waist clanked against the base of his rifle. He had not yet used it on a man, and his bayonet had only been used to clear vines or to pierce the breasts of waterfowl or to decapitate snakes, venomous or otherwise. Regardless, on those occasions he had been able to eat. With each step, he had the thought, *I can go no farther.* Each time, he took one more step. Emotionally weakened, it did not occur to Takashi to assume that every single man who marched alongside him was stricken with the same weaknesses and the same thoughts. Tired as he was, each time that damn canteen struck against his thigh, he nearly wailed in agony, but weakness held his pain captive, and so he endured his hardship in silence, just like the rest of them.

"I don't have the strength to keep writing this. To go on living with this feeling is painful beyond description. Isn't there someone kind enough to strangle me in my sleep?"

Now that Takashi understood the words that his father had written, he lacked the strength to weep.

"…neither his situation nor his physical energy would permit him to keep this up. He grew gradually weaker, like the tree Swift saw so long ago, withering from the top down."

— Ryūnosuke Akutagawa,
The Life of a Stupid Man

"I am afraid because I can so clearly foresee my own life rotting away of itself, like a leaf that rots without falling, while I pursue my round of existence from day to day. That is what I find impossible to bear…"

— Osamu Dazai,
The Setting Sun

IX

The Grand Sagacity
of Every Spirit

THE COMMAND to break ranks and rest for the night was given once they'd reached a bank of trees. For Takashi, this was rather literal: even in his exacerbated state of exhaustion and near starvation, sleep made itself scarce, and so he had only the strength required to lie down. The physical reserves necessary to quiet his mind were not present. He recalled his father screaming in the night, "Sleep is a paradise! Sleep is a paradise! I've been condemned to hell!" and feeling as though he'd heard something entirely inappropriate. The next morning, Ryūnosuke had appeared cheerful, the skin beneath his eyes tinged with deep blue even as he laughed with his children in the light of morning.

Night had fallen near the Sing River, and cicadas could be heard over the artillery that resounded in the distance, although its volume was beginning to diminish. The mountain range that lay ahead concealed the fierce blasts, although the jagged ridges of the mountains were faintly illuminated, as though the sky was reflecting the double of the sunset that had earlier granted the men this respite. Beyond it was Meiktila, their destination. Drifting clouds and lingering smoke were indistinguishable in the blistering sprawl of night. These forms of air and shadow draped themselves over the silver moon much like a shroud over a mirror in that antiquated European tradition of mourning still practiced by the middle class in urban Japan.

It was as though God had deserted, or perhaps merely neglected, these men. The cicadas continued their shrill yet melancholy songs, whose echoes filled the valley in a way somehow different than the same sounds in Japan. "Tsuku tsuku bōshi," the insects sang in piercing clarity, ignorant of the sorrow and homesickness they provoked in the hearts of these men simply by their innate behavior. It is the nature of cicadas to sing much as it is the nature of man to suffer. The ringing cries of "tsuku tsuku bōshi" assailed the men in that humid night air perfumed by fragrant grasses and the unnerving sweetness of decay; the scent of gunpowder overpowered all of this. Hayabusa and Mitsubishi engines were nowhere to be heard.

"We've got reserves moving ahead, no?"

"The hell if I know."

"We're too few to be effective, at any rate…"

A loud "Shut up!" was accompanied by a slap.

"Do you think we'll win?"

"Well, they certainly won't take us alive."

"If only we can cut behind them for once, surely we'll recapture Meiktila."

"We'll give 'em hell this time. Just you wait!"

Such were the conversations Sergeant Takashi Akutagawa heard as he listened to the cicadas, doing his best to write a letter in the dimly flickering light, which gave everyone in the palm grove the appearance of jaundice. *We ARE the reserves*, he'd had the impulse to say earlier, stifling himself the moment he'd had the thought, curtailing his innate sarcasm. Takashi had no desire either to demoralize the private who'd spoken so earnestly in naïve hope, or to relieve himself of his frustration by shouting at someone who'd meant him no harm. Or, perhaps, he simply lacked the energy to produce a verbal response. Perhaps, too, he wanted to burn in anger. He was dead sick of walking, and the bones of his feet had begun to protrude in an unsettling way, leaving little flesh to cushion those things he wore that had no business being described as boots. Fastidious as ever, "The French Officer" still appeared less haggard than most of those around him, even as his spirit was unbearably tattered, threatening to unravel.

Beneath the stars, oil lamps revealed shadows of men feverishly unburdening themselves of rifles and whatever else weighed them down, some of them collapsing and using their knapsacks as cushions, nearly unconscious from exhaustion and dropping to the ground much like those who had died and been left behind. Others had not yet lost their strength and so began consuming in haste the mealy rice that few of them bothered to boil. Still others searched the wooded area for tubers, digging with bare fingers and scraps of aluminum from their mess kits; spades had long since been discarded as excess weight. The day had ended, and yet the war continued. Only the sounds of cicadas remained.

The darkness, too, persisted. His letter to Hiroshi completed, Takashi gazed silently, but not vacantly, into the blackness above him, as though expecting some sort of explanation or answer from the cosmos. He received nothing of the sort, only a disquieting apathy that darkened the air beyond the night, beyond reason. On the soil of his homeland, he had dedicated his body and soul to the service of his nation and to the preservation of the emperor. He felt little uneasiness at the prospect of his own death; somehow, he'd lived his life under the assumption that he would face death at a young age.

Takashi could not say for certain whether or not he had yet killed a man. Certainly, he'd fired at British Indian soldiers during skirmishes. Certainly, multiple men had been wounded by his bullets, perhaps mortally, but there was no proof that he'd fired the fatal shots. These vague uncertainties were what kept him up at night, the moon shining boldly above him. He'd quite likely killed men, but he could not identify them. The British Indian men who had perished beneath that bright hail of gunfire, those shrieking torrents of lead, had been anonymous; in the aftermath, the Japanese men who lay dead or dying around him had disturbed him far more profoundly than the prospect of his having caused the deaths of strangers. He could not forget their cries, which lacked any traces of either falsehood or logic. Those bloodied faces had been those of individuals. Their names, ranks, and particular temperaments, he'd known. This man from Gifu, that one from Wakayama, himself from Tokyo… It's a terrifying thing, seeing a man alive one minute and dead the next. Their eyes soon clouded over like those of gutted fish sold by street vendors, milky and unseeing, their mouths slightly open as though gasping for a final breath. What horrors had they beheld in their final moments? Meanwhile, the scents of blood and exposed viscera lingered in his memories. Takashi harbored no hatred for individuals, but these violent acts that killed his comrades, he thoroughly despised. None of them had any business being here. He did not hate the enemy, only the results of their actions. They had little choice in the matter, he knew, for India was as much a colonial holding as Burma. They were only following orders.

If only he had the option to sleep, to cease this relentless introspection…

This nearly violent intellect that seemed hell-bent on torturing him was, in a cruel twist of either fate or irony, he was unsure which, quite likely the only reason Takashi had survived as long as he had under these inhuman conditions. He was a swift runner, and he was a damn good shot. Yes, individuals, quite likely conscripts like himself, had died, but could he be faulted for having caused the deaths of men far more heavily armed than he? He had not chosen to take up arms against them. With no air support and the anti-tank guns having yet to arrive, the men had been forced to improvise admittedly ingenious methods of blasting enemy tanks. Takashi, especially, had become adept at affixing improvised incendiary devices to the treads of tanks and running to safety before the ersatz missives detonated, shaking the leaves of the palms above him. In doing so, he condemned the men inside to fiery deaths. He simply hoped they died quickly, with little pain.

In his eyes, this war was nothing beyond a vast prison, expressly designed to ruin the lives of an entire generation of young men over petty national ambitions. No, he thought, this was only half true: the victorious would return home to be hailed as heroes, while the defeated would be captured and repatriated only to be regarded as pariahs by those who had never seen a single day of combat, but who nonetheless had strong opinions regarding the war. Quite likely, these opinions would have done an about face since having lost the war, firebrands retreating into the safety of jingoistic pacifism… Somewhere in his heart, Takashi knew he would never return to Japan; like the fallen men whose bodies littered that obscene highway of blood and bones, he knew he would be killed on this soil. No matter how desperately he longed for freedom, there was no escape.

Takashi recalled the words of a friend, an excellent marksman who had been killed by the British regardless, felled a month ago by strafing from a P-47 Thunderbolt. "There's no way we're getting out of here alive. All of us, we have to be prepared for death; every day, we have to wake up knowing that today might be the day we're killed. And they expect us to be grateful for the privilege." Truly, how could these men, subject to the enemy's superior artillery, disease, malnutrition, and outright exhaustion; how could any of them expect to survive, nevermind escape? The deceased corporal had been lucky in his death, as friendly Burmese locals had helped the Japanese soldiers cremate the dead, even going so far as to offer up prayers for the souls of these foreigners. On occasion, they bonded over mutual fear of British strafing and deeply held Buddhist beliefs. Shared faith served as a bond where there should have been animosity. The men of Okami 1872 would often chide each other, "Watch your language!" lest they cause offense to the pious locals who had taken a liking to them.

"Cremate it. Turn it to ashes."

Takashi once again recalled the words of General Nogi, who had perhaps forced himself to view his son as a burnt offering rather than a man as a sort of survival mechanism. The funeral pyres, these mass cremations of the dead who would this time not be left to rot like animals on the roadside, had burned themselves indelibly onto the minds and hearts of these men who were too young to be fathers. Takashi, despite his absence of years, had presently come to understand his own father's simultaneous reverence and revulsion towards the famed general, who had remained alive for thirty-five years despite having risen to tiers of shame and horror unimaginable to most.

Desertion? No, this was no longer an option. Takashi had no intention of branding the name "Akutagawa" as a shameful one; so intense was Nogi's pain that he'd decided against adopting a son to continue the family name that he considered tarnished. Hiroshi and Yasushi still lived, and Takashi could not bear to act in a way that would cause shame to his brothers, or direct the petty attention of the kenpeitai towards his mother. Takashi forced himself against nature into becoming a man of the battlefield.

"Even if it seems certain that you will lose, retaliate. Neither wisdom nor technique has a place in this. A real man does not think of victory or defeat. He plunges recklessly towards an irrational death. By doing this, you will awaken from your dreams."

According to the Hagakure, a man exists for a generation, but his name persists to the end of time. Takashi resigned himself to willful annihilation, much like his father, who had ensured that his sons were raised with an anachronistic level of respect for the traditions of their forefathers even while deriding the social order. In Burma, Takashi was trapped, despair pressing upon him with a frightful strength, and yet he felt the stirrings of something like pride. He, the son of a poet, had faced down machine guns; he, the introverted student of French poetry, had charged forward even when surrounded by bloodshed and destruction. He had survived up until this point, that much was certain, but at what cost?

"There, his human value shines a beautiful light. His human exaltation, which he did not regret even as a soldier, won the final victory in the judgment of truth."

— Corporal Chikushiro Oka,
on Takashi Akutagawa

"We had no ammunition, no clothes, no food, no guns… The men were barefoot and ragged, and threw away everything except canes to help them walk. Their eyes blazed in their lean bodies… All they had to keep them going was grass and water… At Kohima we were starved and then crushed."

— Shizuo Maruyama,
war correspondent

X

The Sheer Intensity of Spirit

IN JULY OF 1944, the Burma road was momentarily silent, producing a morbidly discordant effect. Now that the blinding red sun was about to disappear behind the mountainous horizon, the sapphire bright sky was streaked with pale gold, resembling an ocean. Takashi recalled seeing such an ocean, frigid and yet brilliantly colored, when he and Hiroshi had spent a week in Hokkaido several years ago. Lately, everything he saw called to mind memories of Japan, which had grown increasingly dim, as though veiled by a faint mist. Rose-colored clouds drifted across the sky in solemn languor, and soon the fragile peace was once again disturbed by the echoes of shelling in the distance. Once again, no Hayabusa or Mitsubishi engines could be heard. Promoted by the heavy metallic sounds that alternately shrieked and groaned, as though the air itself was in pain, birds fled the extravagant sweeps of palm fronds that lined the path, which was mercifully flat, even if rocky. The shadows of the palms overlapped the shadows of the soldiers who marched with dead eyes, the narrow lines eventually converging into a pool of deepest grey on this soil of Burma. A fragrant spring wind brought with it the scents of gunpowder and scorched petroleum, which briefly disrupted the competing scents of sweat and decay. It was rumored that some of the oil fields had been burnt, although information was scarce. Once again, the guns were silent, and the small green birds returned to the sharply tipped leaves that gleamed golden in the sunset. The sun, too, made its desertion in silence. A fallen branch of a date palm fell to the earth, resulting in a sharp cracking sound wholly distinct from the now silent artillery. A skinny man whose name Takashi had not learned darted towards it, tearing into the overripe flesh of the plum-colored fruit with teeth that were surely loose in their sockets from starvation. The other men scarcely noticed. By now, it was a common occurrence for men to simply drop to the ground, leaden; this one, with the strength and wherewithal to reach sustenance, this miraculous will to survival, would soon rejoin the ranks of those who lived.

Takashi was too weary to notice such movements. Only the sounds of his own footfalls disturbed him. In a state of pronounced ennui, he did his best to recall the face of his mother, lovely and gentle, although her eyes were haunted. In his mind, she appeared in black and white, no different than his father. She, too, was now a ghost to him, a shadow quickly departing from his field of vision; he knew they would only meet again in the afterlife. He pictured a small woman in a black kimono once again holding an oblong box of ashes draped in a sash, dove-white. The old home in Tabata, where he and his brothers had climbed trees and played at swordfighting, where their father had retrieved them from the slanted roof... The retreating sunlight was blinding, but it was glorious. Takashi recalled those days when he had lingered in the newsprint-scented shadows of the Maruzen bookstore, pleasantly chilled and hidden from the stench of humanity. De Maupassant, Baudelaire, Verlaine, these veritable flowers of the fin de siècle that lined the glossy wooden shelves of the top floor had held endless appeal to the youthful romantic. Soon, too, he discovered Gustavo Adolfo Bécquer and François de La Rouchefoucauld, bettering the instruction of his father.

"All of life is not worth a single line of Baudelaire..." his father had famously mused, coldly gazing down upon the forms he deemed shabby and pathetic.

"On neither the sun, nor death, can a man look fixedly," de La Rochefoucauld had written.

Nearby, a man gasped, disrupting Takashi's half-bored musing. Those thoughts were too distant to be called reminiscence. The sound of a human form falling to the ground was hardly different from a sack of rice being dropped, and just as inanimate and dull. A man had fallen to the side of the road, and another had rushed to his side, although he was hardly able to hold up that skeletal form, even with the aid of a makeshift walking stick. A trickle of blood was visible on his forehead; evidently he'd skinned it when he fell, although he showed no appearance of having noticed this, his eyes bleary as he limped along supported by his comrade. That flaming sunlight caused the blood to glisten, and soon the sun had set completely, leaving the men in silent darkness. The scent of blood and sweat remained, mixed with the aldehyde fragrance of the foliage. It was as though the realm of the living had deserted them with the breeze. Even so, they continued marching. In the night, they were free from the threat of enemy strafing, and so they were forced to advance, this army of skeletons.

Beneath the moonlit darkness, the evening shadows had grown to monstrous lengths, like phantoms, evanescent. Takashi's thoughts were reduced to abstractions in his exhaustion. Because he could not regret, he sorrowed. Did he have a desire for regret? He pitied this creature he'd become, but his was a pity without scorn. The choice to continue walking was a deliberate one, although he could not say where that thought originated. It was as though emotion propelled him; only momentum carried him forward. He was soon stricken with a sense of isolation, even though surrounded by others. They gave him the impression of being in the grips of a similar sort of isolation. Takashi had no dreams of victory or glory; existence itself was victory, or perhaps something more akin to martyrdom.

The sound of a grenade bursting in the distance attracted the attention of some of the men, but this was not a cause for alarm or, indeed, much concern at all. The sound of hollow flesh hitting the ground followed, as if artificially delayed in reaction. No flash of illumination could be seen. Quite likely, it was a suicide. The distant nature of the explosion made it clear that the deceased was of some other division, perhaps the Yoshida Corps, which was supposedly nearby. These incidents were occuring with greater frequency the further the emaciated men advanced; the more their supplies dwindled, the fewer men remained to deplete them. Many of the men who detonated their own grenades had not yet lost their mental acuity, and while secure in their presence of mind, chose bloody, instantaneous death. This was done both to end the individual's suffering as well as to relieve the division of a potential burden. Before the decisive action occured, the man on the precipice of suicide would typically give those closest to him whatever money or valuables he had with him. On occasion, two men would share a grenade in a horrifically modern interpretation of traditional shinjū, or double suicide, removing all beauty from the typically poetic act that was so often the subject of kabuki dramas. For those too mentally weakened to choose such a decisive fate, sometimes a trusted friend would provide them with a grenade and gently make a suggestion, "For your own good," with a sorrowful smile. These could best be described as mercy killings done in desperation to reduce the pain of those they now considered closer than family; whichever comrade had supplied that instrument of voluntary death would continue, stoic through his tears. The bodies of those dead men had been abandoned, certainly, but in the end, their souls were loved. When the option presented itself, a lock of hair or the bone of a finger would be clipped to be sent home to Japan for cremation. One day, they would meet again at the Yasukuni Shrine.

Takashi, the son of Japan's most famous suicide, wondered if he, too, would soon face such a decision. Of the three Akutagawa sons, he was the one who most resembled the deceased patriarch in appearance, temperament, and talent. This was the source of increasingly black though droll banter among the division, the fate of "Akutagawa Sensei." Already, Takashi was thinner than some of the men who had chosen to unburden themselves of life, and yet he somehow managed to persist in this march towards death. The grenade in his knapsack continued to remind him of this disquieting fact. Even so, in his reflection, he could only see his father in the last year of his life, doomed and haunted. Nature, for example, had become more beautiful to him than ever, and yet it was now possessed of a beauty that had lost all sense of meaning. The beauty of nature was presently nothing beyond a setting for suffering and death. Was this to be his destiny? Much like his father, was he born only to suffer until death? Although thoughts of pulling the pin on that contemptible grenade flashed through his mind with startling clarity, these thoughts were artificially planted there; had he not heard that explosion and subsequent collapse of flesh, he quite likely would not have had such thoughts. These thoughts of voluntary death were externally imposed, rather than the result of any internal stirrings. Takashi's desire was not for death, even if his demise, voluntary or otherwise, seemed to be a certainty. In this, he differed from his father.

"I do not know when I will summon up the resolve to kill myself. But nature is for me more beautiful than it has ever been before. I have no doubt that you will laugh at the contradiction, for here I love nature even when I am contemplating suicide. But nature is beautiful because it comes to my eyes in their last extremity."

Their terminal labyrinth…

Takashi could not laugh at the contradictions presented by his father. He could only sigh in sympathy, resigned. He was uncertain how many suicide notes his father had written, perhaps a dozen, but this phrasing was in one of them, and he presently understood his father's heart in a way that quite frankly disturbed him. For two years, he, too, had seen nature with his eyes in their last extremity; however he be brought to his death, his final memories would be those of unrestrained beauty, even if such beauty was to be stripped to its barest components, acoustic.

If desirous of survival, an infantryman should glimpse nature only through the lense of the essential; beauty was now endowed with the element of trite necessity. Splendor was emboldened by utility. The soft curve of a riverbed would be transformed into a shelter from enemy gunfire, or an irritating obstacle for the gun-carriages whose wheels continued to clatter over roughly hewn stones in the night. Vast fields of flowering grasses, too, were reduced to nothing beyond terrain that would place the men at risk of enemy strafing in the daylight, and so could be traversed only in darkness. In war, nature had lost her purity, but a certain hostile beauty remained in its stead. White had been stained with crimson.

"And if you're captured?"

"That'll never happen…" was audible in a Kyūshū accent, dynamic and stubborn; cocky, even.

"They think being a prisoner of war is brave, an honor. Ha! Glorious capture, what bullshit. 'You boys fought hard,' they'll say. 'There's no shame in surrender,' they'll say…"

"Easy for them to say."

"A samurai has no business surrendering."

A light rain had begun to fall as if to punctuate these wholeheartedly spoken remarks. Without so much as a glance at his watch, whose continued function was nothing short of miraculous considering the climate, Takashi instinctively knew that it was well after midnight. Mirroring the eccentric habit of his father, he counted his footsteps; repetition of mental action such as this calmed his nerves. Yet again, he was forced to concentrate on that idea of death, of the cessation of his own existence. "Never again will I walk along this path. Never again will I take these steps," Takashi thought. "Never again will I see Japan." Doubtless, all of the men were having similar thoughts, even if buried beneath a comfortable shield of braggadocio. Takashi, having grown accustomed to mortality at an age when most were concerned with nothing beyond schooling and petty scuffles with siblings, could confront these thoughts directly. He had no use for the softening of abrupt truth. Without fear, he stared into the eyes of death, those silent pools of black oblivion.

Takashi forced his consciousness into the wholehearted pursuit of the awareness of the gravity of the present moment. This was an unnatural sort of awareness. His entire life had been nothing but a succession of such moments; indeed, was that not the fate of man? Takashi lived with the misfortune of being cognizant of the repetitive nature of such moments. Left with nothing beyond the thoughts that darkened his mind, with no diversions, he had no other avenues to pursue. He threw his entire being into the singular purpose of the moment. This was the nature of the bushi, that ancient warrior's spirit with which he'd been raised.

"Absence diminishes mediocre passions and increases great ones, as the wind extinguishes candles and fans fires." Takashi no longer had any books with him, but he had long ago committed the words of de La Rouchefoucauld to the haven of memory. Left with nothing but memories, Takashi found respite in the language he knew by heart.

Never again would he walk down this road built by the dead that stretched through floodplains and mountains that formed this beautiful, foreign terrain called Burma. Something about this seemed eerie, uncanny even. In Japan, even if in an unfamiliar area, this presentiment of strangeness never came to him. He attributed this to the knowledge that, when he'd been in Japan, there was always the potential to return to any given area. Wherever in Japan he visited, the atmosphere was lightened by the nebulous possibility known as "future." Here, such potential was absent; the darkness, the endless marching, this was the future made manifest in the present. Although they lived in Tokyo, he and Hiroshi could always visit their auntie in Hokkaido; any number of times, he had the option of spending a week on the Izu peninsula with his classmates in the French club, invariably being teased that he and his father preferred the same geisha. To the amusement of everyone, he would give vent to this lighthearted frustration during school kendo tournaments. Taller than most of them and a natural talent, he disliked the sport.

"Akutagawa! Wasn't it your father who said an artist should also be a martial artist? Art without action is impotent, or somesuch?" the middle-aged kendo instructor would say. Sullen, Takashi would avert his eyes. Whichever student was unlucky enough to be subsequently pitted against him would be the recipient of an angry thrashing with a bamboo sword. Indeed, the other students would fix the matches so as not to be pitted against this reluctant victor.

* * *

"Unload all the bullets from your rifles" was the command, tersely delivered in a low tone.

From repeated drills and the sobering hell of experience, the men had quickly learned that the bayonet was the ideal defense weapon when subjected to attacks in the night. Dawn was not yet near, and the sounds of insects and exotic birds abruptly became silent. The forest they'd reached gave the impression of being haunted.

Earlier, they had been walking, rather than marching, preparing to rest for a few hours before the sun rose. Another division was ahead of them, and so the men of Okami 1872 had been given no reason to anticipate an ambush. Above them, the stars gleamed the color of platinum, and Takashi's mind once again wandered to the skies above his mother country. These stars seemed to burst as gunfire rang out. Flashes of gold exploded in the darkness, illuminating the silence, and the men dropped to the ground like marionettes whose strings had been severed by a sword. Relaxation was replaced with the taut precision of condensed motion. Voices could be heard in English.

"Over here! To the left!"

Fighting would surely commence within a few minutes. Takashi, the interpreter, forced himself to be silent; he could not see who was next to him, but he slapped the man on the arm and furtively gestured to the right, where those foreign words originated. It was quite likely that several of them would die. When Takashi took into account that he could very well be one of them, he felt little distress as he fixed his bayonet to the right. This sense of apathy was something of a relief. Meanwhile, the dispassionate night dimmed all form. The English outnumbered them greatly; even without visibility, this was obvious. Their weapons, too, were better. Indeed, the English had every advantage. It was as though God himself had seen fit to damn these poorly equipped and malnourished men to some inhospitable foreign hell. Much as they surely prayed, heaven did not see fit to lend them support.

The firing began. Flat on the ground, a row of bayonets fixed towards the right, the men were still as death. Palm trees and ferns surrounded them; perhaps the shadows of nature hid the forms of men who lay motionless in a shallow ditch. Branches were felled by the hail of gunfire, hiding the men from view as brilliant flashes of light soared through the air, nearly liquid in quality. Hidden by the fallen leaves, no bayonets were bloodied. The sun rose without incident as the men took their rest beneath the protection of fallen branches. Everything was shrouded in darkness, and Takashi was no longer tormented by consciousness.

"The sound of his enemy's name was not enough
to rouse his lethargic spirit to an active hate."

— Takeo Arishima,
Descendants of Cain

"The coming generations will not so much
accuse us of our mistakes as they will
understand our passion sympathetically."

— Ryūnosuke Akutagawa,
journals, 1927

XI

The Consciousness of His Own Disadvantages

"I'VE UPSET TōJō, I'll probably end up in Burma" had by now become a common saying among generals on the mainland, rumor had it. Although the mail received by these weary men was censored, certain sentiments were implied. From his correspondence with Hiroshi, now a naval officer in that factory on outside of Tokyo, he was able to surmise that men even younger than he were tasked with flying their planes into the decks of enemy ships. Shinpū Tokubetsu Kōgekitai, it was called, "Divine Wind Special Attack Unit." His own brother was tasked with praying over those planes that would carry their pilots to fiery young death. Japan was losing pilots more rapidly than they could train replacements, and he feared Hiroshi would soon be counted among their ranks. Many of these doomed men, superstitious, believed their deaths would relieve their spiritual debt, the accumulated offenses whose reparation burdened their hearts due to ancestral sin. Some of them simply wished to demonstrate the degree of their filial piety and go to what they regarded as glorious death for the emperor.

"At least we're not in the Philippines," Takashi heard as a whisper, conspiratorial in tone. "You don't want to know what they're eating."

The sounds of artillery were no longer frightening to any of them, the fearsome having now become merely commonplace. The memory of the attack in the palm grove was indistinguishable from numerous similar instances, harrowing only in the abstract. No one had been killed. The following day, as they continued their march to certain death, burned-out shells that had once been traditional Burmese houses were visible. Set against the brilliant green of the hillside and the blue, deep and rich, of the rivers, the bone-colored ash gave the impression of obscenity, of blasphemous violation. The Burmese had not asked for either the Japanese or the English to come into this lovely country that was presently being destroyed by interlopers.

This routing to Imphal was abrupt; along the roadside, type 97-Kai Shinhōtō Chi-Ha tanks whose engines were inoperable or that had simply run out of fuel had been sunk into the soil as artillery, ironically serving as anti-tank guns against the English.

Okami 1872 continued to advance in the direction of Imphal. Carefully, they continued to move forward, surrounded by this ersatz artillery, the sight of which incited a certain majesty tinged with the melancholy of ruin. With no warning, several English tanks appeared much like the faint outlines of ships upon a placid horizon. The men dropped to the ground, and the Japanese "guns" began to send out a steady hail of fire above them. Alongside the English tanks were trucks; evidently, they had been carrying petroleum, perhaps taken from one of the Burmese oil fields that had since been burned, for they went up in massive curtains of flame. Takashi saw what could best be described as something resembling the pillar of fire spoken of in Exodus; the effect was terrific in every sense of the word. There was no freedom to be found in this landscape, despite the glorious optics. The flat topography offered no shelter, and so the men were helpless and could only stare in awe at the sight before them, having received no orders to return fire.

The English tanks, as if intentionally tormenting them, returned fire. The fierce rounds had found their targets in several of the men, although too few in number to be the cause of much concern. There was a Burmese village nearby that had not been burned; the ardently Buddhist residents would undoubtedly be grateful to aid the men in the cremation of the fallen young men who had shared their faith. To say that the scenario was staunchly in favor of the English would be an understatement; the situation was far too ridiculous to cause any of them to feel forlorn. Helpless and trapped, they could not move, and many prayers went up that the English would be too fearful of deaths caused by those exploding trucks to continue in their fire.

The English were fortunate to have superior weapons and superior manpower; the sole advantage held by the Japanese was the lack of a fear of death.

"Hangekisuru!"

The order to fire, to strike back, was made only once the tanks had begun to retreat. This was due to the shortage of bullets. Alongside the others, Takashi aimed his rifle at the dozen or so men who surrounded the tanks that had begun to move in the opposite direction. The flames from the burning trucks, despite the distance of perhaps half a kilometer, stung his eyes, and still his aim did not waver. The ground itself was hot; the sun had heated the soil and stones much like a kiln for firing ceramics, and the valley seemed expressly designed to trap such heat, and the beauty of nature became a flaming hellscape. He only noticed this after firing several rounds. The "anti-tank guns" continued to fire overhead. Some of the men hurled grenades, while others fired machine guns.

As though fainting, several of the Englishmen dropped to the ground, much like the Japanese who had perished from exhaustion on the Burma road.

"Man down! Man down!" Takashi heard in an impassioned sort of English. He then heard something in an incomprehensible language, perhaps some sort of Punjabi dialect. The Gurkhas they especially feared.

The Japanese had no such need to signal the death of an individual. The English, it seemed, did their best to manage their fear of death; the Japanese simply lacked this animal fear, flatly rejecting anything resembling a sentimental attachment to life for its own sake.

"Cease fire!" Takashi shouted in flawless English.

The English completed their retreat, having taken at least as many casualties as Okami.

* * *

The route to Imphal was called the Yasukuni Road, despite no battle having yet occurred. In this moment of irreversible momentum, Takashi was left with the impression that he had passed over into a savage world from which there was no return. No one could have known what he had seen, done, and thought during that perilous time; his existence, his "survival" continued on as the result of a sequence of nearly supernatural chance occurrences. Perhaps his father was guarding him. In his memory, those words in rudely spoken English echoed. "Man down! Man down!" His own voice, so similar to that of his father… Had Takashi been shot, no one would have shouted the equivalent in his mother tongue. This caused him no distress.

In every conceivable way, this landscape was another world. Takashi could not distance himself from the voices of the enemy that had once resounded around him and presently continued in his mind as the men continued their march towards certain destruction. He had not seen many of them. This was in equal parts due to the haze of gunfire as well as the deliberate aversion of his vision; were he to see the eyes of a man he had killed, he feared he would never be spared the eternal gaze of the blind eyes of the dead; even with this fear, he imagined the English dead were less vengeful than the Japanese dead. Still, he'd glimpsed them in formation, and he used this composite image to forge those vaguely defined features into something coherent. Those English soldiers had been tall and well-built, their cheeks rosy and full. Regardless of his lack of animosity towards them, Takashi felt a faint sort of spite prickling beneath his skin. Their gratuitous vitality seemed expressly designed to taunt the physically and spiritually depleted Japanese. The English voices, too, had been incongruously lively. His face gaunt and his voice entirely without warmth, Takashi had screamed, "Cease fire!" and his words had been given value by the actions of the enemy. Thanks to the instruction of his deceased father, his English was indistinguishable from that of an Oxford don. This scream by a frail Japanese man, bereft of either hope or fear, the English soldiers had heeded in equal regard to the cry of "Man down!" in a stout cockney accent. Using nothing more than words, lives had undoubtedly been saved. Perhaps Takashi himself had been spared, he thought bitterly as the English made their retreat.

What was this perilous optimism that the Westerners seemed so intent on preserving? The Japanese had the benefit of the certainty of death; the English were forced to live with the uncertainty of their existence. Somehow, they'd seemed at peace with such precarious uncertainty. The certainty of death Takashi found preferable. Perhaps it was an especially private sort of divine retribution that forced onto Takashi the thoughts that would be unbearable for most men; was his fate to be like that of his father, to be prematurely killed by his own intellect after a prolonged period of emotional torture? He lived constantly with death; at any moment, his existence had the potential to be emptied of meaning. His own survival was meaningless.

In the distance, the cawing of peacocks could be heard, catlike and shrill and yet not in the least unpleasant. Bright cries rose with the mist. The faint light of dawn made itself seen; the air took on the translucent quality of the milky way itself. The clouds threatened rain.

Beneath the darkening skies, Takashi's eyes remained unclouded even as his strength began to fail. Some days, even breathing was an ordeal. On others, the beauty of nature left him breathless. As his physical condition deteriorated, he could only feel a heady sort of reverence when his eyes confronted the majesty around him. Even in ruin, the emerald splendor of what man had neither created nor destroyed made itself visible to his tired eyes. Writing was no longer a luxury afforded to him. He'd written to Hiroshi for paper, and there was none to be had; while discouraging, this was unsurprising. Takashi's innate pessimism reduced all expectations, leveling whatever vestiges of hope he had previously had the ability to feel, and so was left with little to lift his flagging spirits. Emotional reactions, too, were a luxury denied to him by the relentless present He was certain both his and Hiroshi's letters were being censored.

The rationing of paper and other similar luxuries, such non-essential niceties that lent polish to an otherwise bland existence, was by now well-known to the men whose trajectory led them down the heavily trod stretch of barren soil so derisively called Yasukuni Road. This profound sense of deprivation even the censors lacked the power to suppress. Especially in Tokyo people suffered; once again, Takashi feared for his mother. People were starving. With Hiroshi and Takashi pressed into service and Yasushi likely soon to receive his notice of conscription for the price of one sen, five rin, she likely had few joys in her solitude. Japan had the paper to print those damn penny postcards and yet there was no stationary for a poet and artist to write a note of encouragement to a woman who was far too young to have been widowed for what would soon amount to seventeen years. Surely the royalties from *The Collected Works of Ryūnosuke Akutagawa* would enable her to endure the hardship with minimal discomfort, Sergeant Takashi Akutagawa thought, at once tearful and derisive. Those same works that were so famous, though, those beautifully wrought words that never risked sentimentality, that was the prose that was most savagely curtailed by the censors. There was a fair chance that certain bookshops would be reluctant to carry them, being understandably unwilling to risk censure by the notoriously petty and unilaterally reviled kenpeitai. Their uniforms had certainly never been soiled by foreign terrain… Because of those men, who more resembled sharply uniformed bureaucrats than police, Hiroshi had written on a creased sheet of Maruzen paper heavily streaked with lines of black ink, and some of their father's friends had ceased writing. Jun'ichirō Tanizaki had sequestered himself in Kyoto, exiling himself to his classically styled domicile in the old capital and translating *The Tale of Genji* into modern Japanese. His novel *Sasameyuki* had been deemed insufficiently patriotic, and so Takashi assumed this arduous project was undertaken to compensate for a perceived lack of passion for the war effort. The novelist Kafū Nagai, friend of both Takashi's late father and the very much alive Tanizaki, had ceased writing entirely in protest. He and Takashi shared a love of French literature, and the older writer's spirit was certainly in keeping with the land of Voltaire. Meanwhile, France, too, had by all accounts lost all sense of such poetic virtue; Germany was certainly no longer the land of Goethe. Meanwhile, the Americans, those so-called lovers of freedom, would have eagerly thrown these heirs of Murasaki into concentration camps due to their heredity.

In his mind, Takashi began composing what he called a phantom novel, his words being lent spirit in his heart. These words would never be written, but they were certainly alive in his mind; beyond alive, they were vibrant. Especially at moments of crisis, his mind indulged in thoughts that were thoroughly unimportant and therefore all the more interesting. Across his ashen face fell a stray beam of light emanating from the east, resplendent in its flame-colored aura; this light was filtered through the narrow, serrated branches of palms that had long since been stripped bare of fruit by both the men who marched upon the soil and the birds swept aloft by the breeze. For a moment, there was no tension between Takashi's patriotic duty and his wounded conscience. In the faint glow of morning, war was no longer merely a matter of defeat or of victory, of surrender or of suicide… Death would serve as a substitute for victory, a spiteful sort of glory. In war, the entirety of the subconscious workings of mankind displayed itself on a grand scale, and the dramatis personae staked their lives on this performative justice. Selfish designs, fickle emotions, and blind egoism revealed qualities of humanity that would be deemed crass in

"Was it death he was waiting for? Or a wild ecstasy
of the senses? The two seemed to overlap almost as
if the object of bodily desire was death itself. But,
however that might be, it was certain that never before
had the lieutenant tasted such total freedom."

— Yukio Mishima,
"Patriotism"

"What would be would be; I would stand up
to fate, although it might keep torturing me
despite every attempt to find a way out."

— Naoya Shiga,
"Han's Crime"

XII

The Sword of the Mind

TAKASHI'S loneliness was of such strength that he could no longer use either reason or faith to will it away, and so it clung to him like a withered shroud. As the men, famished and exhausted, took refuge in a burned-out village shortly before the dawn, the air itself seemed to carry with it a sort of sorrow too plaintive to be expressed. The thoughts that occupied Takashi's mind were morose, even bordering on the obsessive. Should fate deign to treat him with such malice, thrashing him at every opportunity, even finding more than nature should allow, then so may be it. Coldly, he deemed fate as something never to be trusted. For nearly two years, he had thought only of a death that had not yet come but was rapidly encroaching.

"Oh God, oh God, why hast thou forsaken me; far from my salvation, my roaring words." Certainly, death would be easier; at least there would be no more uncertainty. The familiar words of Psalm XXII offered something nearing comfort and yet sadly short of peace, nevermind enlightenment. Quite likely, the English soldiers that had been killed knew the words just as well as this Japanese man. None of them would assume this man from the East to know the words of David, Takashi assumed without the slightest hint of malice. Cicadas sang in the moonless darkness that stretched beyond the mountains, whose peaks pierced the banks of cloud that swirled above. No artillery or engines could be heard. Somehow, this was disquieting, and

101

the sounds of nature seemed ominous when they would otherwise have been tranquil. "Deliver my soul from the sword of the mind…" Exhaustion engulfed him.

Yet again unable to sleep despite a relentless fatigue coupled with his usual ennui, Takashi did his best to pull himself together by focusing on a certain goal: if death was to be a certainty, then he would do his damndest to ensure that his death was not to be one without meaning. "Akutagawa's death was pointless," a certain naturalist critic had written about his father, whose death had punctured the end of the Taishō era. Takashi recalled many similar hooks written by reporters and critics hoping to capitalize on the death of Japan's foremost literary prodigy. "Tokio Novelist, Tired of Life, Takes Poison," the *New York Times* had written. However, Ryūnosuke Akutagawa had never written a novel… Much like his father, Takashi felt far too keenly the spiritual impoverishment of a world that discarded him with little thought and gave even less consideration to him as an individual.

That morning, British-Indian tanks had come straight towards Okami 1872, firing while skirmishers positioned on the pockmarked slopes of the mountain shot at them in tandem with the heavy caliber shells that ripped open the soil. While they remained unafraid, the spray of bullets, shrieking much like the cicadas, prevented them from taking aim at anything, not that their rifles would have been of much use. Presently, the rifles were more useful as walking sticks.

One tank had come quite close to them, but the steep angle of the riverbed had spared them. Regardless, the experience was harrowing; even if death was no longer a fearsome prospect, having the treads of a tank come so near one's face was a monstrous thing to endure, a waking nightmare. For hours, they were trapped in that dried-up ditch. A few of the men, delirious from thirst, perhaps hallucinating, climbed out to find water despite the shouts of comrades. Perhaps they'd not heard them at all. All of them were gunned down; it seemed as though these British-Indian soldiers, they knew not yet which regiment, had an endless supply of ammunition and nothing better to do than expend it on starving men. On occasion, the Japanese were able to hurl coconut shells filled with gunpowder and rigged with fuses at the tanks; this was no longer a possibility.

Several hours passed. Takashi could no longer delineate the borders of reality, having become lost in the crazed sounds like the wings of so many whirring insects. He lived on instinct alone. The shadows cast by trees that had been stripped of leaves grew longer, pitiful and thin. In the distance, a low rumbling could be heard.

"Banzai!"

One after another, cries went up from the men whose legs were cramped due to hours of forced immobility, their skin drenched in perspiration and darkened by dust. It was just past noon, and Japanese tanks had finally arrived, beginning a close-range attack. Mortars began to explode around the enemy tanks, which began to retreat as though bored.

"Banzai! Banzai!"

The enemy tanks having retreated, the surviving men gathered the dead and wounded, carrying them on stretchers as far as they could. The dead were cremated at what remained of a village perhaps a quarter of the way up the mountain; prayers in Japanese and Burmese went up to the heavens for their souls alongside silvery plumes of smoke. Even so, none of these men would get posthumous names, their ashes forever to reside on foreign soil. For the survivors, only exhaustion remained. Fortunately, the night passed without event, and soon the sun reached the position the moon had not occupied in that blackest night without illumination.

* * *

Upon his conscription, Takashi's right to live, or what could perhaps better be described as his right to not be killed, was stripped from him. The usual codes preventing societal collapse did not apply on the battlefield; if he was to be shot, his killer would certainly not be tried as a murderer. Few outside his family would care. The man who fired the fatal shot would only be considered a man who had performed dutifully in the service to the land of his birth. The fatal actions would perhaps even be rewarded, should the shooter survive and return to whichever nation had seen fit to send him to these abject conditions. War is something that both transcends and destroys individual interests.

I refuse to seek peace in resignation, Takashi thought, agitated, the words now awkward and somewhat forced in his mind. Peace was nowhere to be found in those thoughts that were as impenetrable as the vine-choked thickets that concealed the 49th Division from the enemy. "Refuse to give in. Go to your death without regrets." Once again, the words were forced; his present state of mind, this peculiar mental landscape, was entirely unnatural for one whose haughty artistic inclinations had been nurtured from childhood.

"Anyone who regards literature as his life cannot be satisfied with the beautiful alone… Indeed, to be an artist, he must take everything in stride, nervous breakdown, insanity, and even prison," his father had been told by the sensei who had died six years before Takashi's birth. Being an infantryman, then, was its own particular form of artistry. Takashi dedicated himself to cultivating this art to its utmost limits. Much like his father, it would certainly result in his destruction; similarly, he feared insanity. All of the things he had seen and experienced… Even amidst the savage panorama of carnage and decay that trapped him, beauty still did not desert his vision. Could this, then, be called madness? This was all so thoroughly abnormal when compared to life in civilized society. What was society, though, but a battlefield where no blood was spilled, a front without the prospect of glory? Perhaps, then, the unhuman things Takashi had seen during his time in these jungles and on that godforsaken road paved with corpses were far more natural than the odd balance of hierarchies and minutiae that allowed society to function. At least in war, the hierarchy was clearly, even if bluntly, delineated.

Such, then, were Takashi's thoughts, which he had neglected as of late, their depths having been reduced to a state of formless static imagery after multiple skirmishes and extended deprivation of basic human dignities. Much like his rifle, the hinges that allowed his thoughts to click so neatly into place seemed to have rusted over. The humid climate suited neither the rifle nor his temperament. Now paranoid, these thoughts haunted him even, or perhaps especially, before he had been able to articulate them in his "phantom novel." Left without paper, his philosophy became crystallized in his mind.

"It is natural that all men should die, and yet few despair about this daily; indeed, such inevitabilities scarcely interrupt the flow of thoughts in the minds of most, and so death is an unobtrusive force that irrevocably shapes modern society. Most men pay no mind to infinity. Some despair at the prospect of their own demise, while others force such thoughts into oblivion, ignoring them entirely. On occasion, death retreats from thought like some great tidal force; in times of war, death makes its presence felt in such monstrous torrents that no amount of patriotic anthems can drown out. No species but humanity knows that its destiny is to struggle until death, and so no one but man makes an attempt to defy this fate, to resist these tides with his own blood. Precious few acknowledge this inevitability, even as their gut instincts propel them to take whatever measures possible to prolong life. The blindness of will is certainly a damned stubborn thing…"

Takashi wanted more than anything to understand that blind will to live, that animal strength, and yet such a state remained elusive. He was not desirous of death, only of a peace that he would never know. For the entirety of his service, he had felt as though countless shadows had surrounded him, their objectives as vague as the outlines of the trees whose branches stretched above him in the dawn. What were these phantoms, urging him on? He felt no need to deny his own fate. On this immutable trajectory, he longed to see what no living man had seen, to feel in his heart the things denied to all of those who would survive. This caused him no fear. As a matter of course, it was the nature of life to perish; only man struggled against this, and similarly, only man hastened his own demise.

"If the time comes when I have to take up the gun,
I will be happy to die for the nation. I can conceive
of no resolution beyond that, nor do I think one
necessary. Taking up the gun as a man of letters
makes no sense. All who fight, fight as soldiers."

— Hideo Kobayashi,
'On War'

XIII

Perennial Tears
Descend in Gems

"IF I RETURN to Japan, I suppose I'll find my grave there…"
The low voice was unfamiliar, but it could have been spoken by any one of the men in Takashi's company. It seemed to him that nothing could be more abject than poverty of the spirit, but he could not describe himself as spiritually impoverished. "Robbed" or perhaps "denied" would better serve his descriptive purposes for this omnipresent mire of the soul in which he found himself trapped. The Burmese were a people of deeply held faith; even as their villages were demolished by shelling from the Japanese and the English, and now apparently the Americans, it was rumored, most of the locals were no less devout than the itinerant monks that they passed, placid in the purity of their faith. Despite his own hunger, Takashi was still grateful for the increasingly rare occasions in which he could share his rations with them and practice his conversational Burmese. How odd, he thought: this language he would never speak on his home soil. Far more friends than he cared to recall had already died in successively violent manners. Already, there had been many suicides. Some had pulled the pins on their grenades as they clutched them to their hearts, while others had hanged themselves with their belts. Many had died in combat or

simply vanished. Now, as the survivors neared a small Burmese village without a name, white-robed mendicants could pray for their souls.

From what little that could be gathered from the stations that reached the badly damaged radio, the war was rather one-sided, although no one dared say this explicitly without copious amounts of saké, of which they had in greater quantities than food. Supply lines had broken down, and the Japanese troops were destitute. Three years earlier, when the decision had been made to bomb the Americans, the Japanese had appeared invincible, the average soldier having been trained in the fashion of the prototypical Nietzschean overman. Presently, they existed in a state of prolonged collapse. Their uniforms, once bright olive and neatly pressed, were now blackened and tattered. They slept exposed on the earth, their bedding consisting of half-rotten blankets thrown over damp leaves, lacking even mosquito nets in these jungles that reeked of death. Without the obvious being so blatantly stated, the war was over. The only thing in question was how much of this state of listless wandering they would have to endure before a full collapse sealed their fate.

Takashi had long since abandoned, or perhaps discarded, any faith that he'd held in anything short of a brutal defeat at the hands of the English. He dreaded the national humiliation that would undoubtedly result, even if he had no expectations of experiencing it. He feared what his mother and Hiroshi and Yasushi, "Ya-chan," would have to live through should they survive. It was rumored that Tokyo would be bombed, and the aircraft factory "employing" Hiroshi would certainly be an appealing target for American forces. Perhaps Ruriko would, indeed, be a young widow with three children, just like their mother...

Even while bearing this, there was no choice but to press on. Some of the men were suffering from malaria; others had wounds that remained unhealed due to the humidity and stank of yet more rot. Poverty was, indeed, the most adequate description of the collective sorrow faced by those on the losing side of any war. Few miseries could be greater than feeling that one's spirit was utterly without strength, depleted of every vestige of hope and battered even when no provocation had been shown. The despair, though palpable, brought with it a certain morose levity.

"Yes, if I return to Japan, I suppose I'll find my grave there," the same man repeated, following the remark with a dramatic sigh to elicit a response from anyone who cared to do so.

"Idiot. You'll get gunned down by some Yank stinking of milk!"

"I hear General Mutaguchi's so certain of victory at Imphal, he's already ordered a shipload of geisha to be sent over!"

"What bullshit. The same general who left his men with twenty days of food for a four-month campaign... Genghis Khan, my ass."

When en route to an engagement in which they might very well be killed, the men would often chide each other to break the grim silence that enveloped them like a second skin, taut and awkward as it lingered on in seeming perpetuity. Takashi imagined this feeling to be the equivalent of that of a prison inmate sentenced to death: although no date of execution had been set, death was nothing if not an inevitability, and so he was left in pained idleness. Somehow, living under the constant threat of death had taken on a stultifying quality, cloying even. These days were horrible, more hellish than hell itself, as Takashi's father had written many times. Even so, the odd levity was undeniable. Some of the men had begun to weep at the beauty visible only in the dregs of a sunset, greedily devouring the flaming skies when no poetry could be composed. Others fell in love with the Burmese culture, the lukewarm Buddhist sentiments they'd previously harbored ripening into an uncannily purified sort of faith. Still others found a nihilistic peace much in the manner of the protagonists of Turgenev or Chekhov. "What does it matter?" could often be heard. Still, if he avoided falling into the chasm of bloodlust, the average soldier saw beauty even in this inescapable darkness.

"Nothing is more beautiful than the landscape of Japan. Oh, what a splendid country is mine! The sea of deepest green trees, those vast fields of flowering grass...!" No one could say that but a man whose wrists had been shackled by fate, and yet Takashi spoke without reserve in the language of his birth. Emphatic in their agreement, no one called him mad. Such thoughts did not occur to them, for they all harbored the same sentiments.

In the southwest of Burma on the Arakan Peninsula, the combined English and Indian forces had begun retaking land from the Japanese with frightful haste as they pressed towards Rangoon. Meanwhile, in central Burma, General Slim had received word that the Japanese 15th and 33rd divisions were not routed for Mandalay, but rather the town of Meiktila. Slim's forces had subsequently crossed through Shwebo, that old capital of King Alaungpaya with its golden temples in the shadows of the Arakan Mountains. The English were now arrayed near the Irrawaddy in several locations. For some time, the Japanese were closely monitored. General Heitaro Kimura, commanding Japanese forces in the region, was none the wiser. He had served during the Siberian intervention after the Bolshevik uprising, supporting the White Russians against the Red Army; Japan's present fate seemed as dire as that of Imperial Russia and the murdered Tsar, many of the young men remarkably stoic even as they accepted the fates their mother nation had chosen for them. Worn down and and lacking all but the barest of provisions, the Japanese had extended their forces too far beyond the reach of their strained supply lines.

In the spring of 1945, the hills of Burma had the effulgent quality of a Cézanne landscape, pale greens and piercing shades of lapis lazuli resplendent, filtered through rays of delicately stippled sunlight. It was beautiful, even when those rolling hillsides served as little more than repositories for the dead and dying. As he'd thought many times before, the prevalence of death, the excessively grotesque reminders of the transience of life, only magnified this beauty that seemed nearly sculpted in Takashi's eyes. Even amidst these sweeping vistas of death, beauty still had meaning. His father had written a novella about an artist who could only paint what he had seen with his own eyes; tortured by his hideous visions until he had grown cruel, the "demon painter" Yoshihide could only paint scenes of hell. Driven by his demon and obsessed with the perfection of his artistry, Yoshihide, in his sublime madness, was quite obviously symbolic of Ryūnosuke Akutagawa. Takashi, in ways he found disconcerting, now understood his father in a nearly fearsome way. A man out of time, the spirit of the fin de siècle haunted him, and yet he had no complaints. Transcending his own personal tragedy, having been severed from the boundaries separating beauty and horror, he felt something nearing triumph, even as he prepared for what would ultimately result in his destruction. The excessive preparation for death resulted in a sense of invulnerability, even as he found himself feeling so deeply understood by a man who was no longer among the living.

Perhaps this damage was his own form of individualism…

"Paint me something, Ryū-chan!" he or Hiroshi would pester their father. Silently, perhaps with a smirk on his gaunt but famously handsome face as he smoked a Golden Bat cigarette, their father would cease his compulsive writing, take from his notebook a clean sheet of Maruzen paper, and paint something in the sumi-e style brought to Japan from China in the 12ᵗʰ century.

"A ghost!" Hiroshi said, smiling. Takashi, clutching the dove-white paper colored with ink the color of tea, kicked his father's knee beneath the low rosewood desk. Smiling faintly, running his fingers through his long hair, his father took a puff of his cigarette and blew smoke in his second son's direction.

"Ryū-chan looks like a ghost!" Hiroshi exclaimed, dramatically fanning away the fragrant smoke that obscured his father's face.

In Takashi's memory, his father was, indeed, a ghost, his face veiled by mist. As he shook his head mournfully, there was no regret in his face, nor was there any trace of bitterness present in his startlingly clear eyes as he ran his fingers over the fringe of blue-black stubble on his skull. The modernization of Japan had killed his father; the modernization of Japan had led to the Japanese having acquired a thirst for empire, much like England, and occupying multiple neighboring countries. It was America that had forcibly opened the isolationist Japan, forcing her to modernize so haphazardly and driving her mad in the process. This was the reason Takashi had been sent to Burma. The very idea of war hurt him, quite literally, far more deeply than the war with the Russians and later the Great War had wounded his father, shattering any idealism that may have been present in his coldly poetic heart. War hurt many people; certainly, many people were angry, perhaps especially at the way the nation of Japan had gone to pieces. Rather than anger, Takashi now felt a sad sort of acceptance in his grief. He had left school and permanently interrupted his study of French. He could not describe his time in the army as meaningless, though: without this, he would not have known the heart of the father who had died when he was a child. He would not have seen hell. Perhaps he was selfish in these thoughts. Perhaps he simply did not want to acknowledge the sheer uselessness of a part of his life, now integral to his existence, that he had been forced to endure, but he could only marvel at the levels of psychological depth to which he had been brought upon this foreign soil. Much like the Burmese monks in their white robes, Takashi felt as though he'd achieved a painful sort of enlightenment.

A quiet smile came to his face. There were a good deal of men who enjoyed their tenure in the army; it suited many of their natures, even giving many of them a maturity beyond their years. Takashi could not say he enjoyed this, but neither could he deny the effect his service had had upon his character. In that two-story home in Tabata, leisurely translating de La Rouchefoucauld and Verlaine at his father's desk, he'd learned beauty; in Burma, he'd seen firsthand the nightmares that had tormented his father. There were some who could only see the ugliness of the war, but Takashi could say with a clear conscience that he was innocent. He had killed men, certainly, but plenty of them had done their best to kill him as well. He had committed no atrocities, and certainly his experience had been terrible, but without this horror, he could not appreciate the beauty that surrounded him. Without having seen hell, the beauty of heaven would have no meaning. More than ever, he loved his father.

Takashi tried in vain to fall asleep. He longed to empty his mind of everything. Again and again, he did his best to extinguish the thoughts that lingered in his consciousness like dying embers; even pleasant memories were now burning torments. Perhaps this insomnia, this deficiency, was a strength in these conditions that had already induced madness in many of the men. Even as a student, there were many nights when Takashi would sleep no more than an hour, worries about his studies or idle thoughts about the pleasant weather hammering at him. The grandfather clock in the hallway would chime midnight, then one, then two, then three... He would be assaulted anew with worries about a history examination, or thoughts on Japan's political situation, or a pleasant recollection of a flirtatious waitress on the Ginza, with Hiroshi elbowing him in the ribs afterwards. Each remembrance he'd brushed aside, and each time new thoughts continued to hammer away at him, renewing their attacks with untiring persistence. These thoughts never would turn to ash...

Beneath a canopy of low branches heavy with morning dew, already as dense as a light spray of raindrops, there was no sound of a clock. This precipitation, at least, served as a discouragement for the mosquitoes. Takashi could not free himself from his thoughts, and so he decided to yield to them, letting them flood him until they spent themselves and ran dry.

"I'm so hungry... I'm so hungry, I can't sleep."

When it had still been night, Takashi had heard those words; he'd recognized the voice, that of a student draftee much like himself, who had previously fought with the 54th Division. Earlier in the year, the corporal had been far more robust than Takashi, both physically and temperamentally. Now, starving and shell-shocked, the corporal was reduced to weeping in the night, gorging himself on water to assuage his pangs of hunger. Perhaps all of the weaknesses that Takashi had inherited from his father only served to prolong his life that would otherwise have been crushed beneath these unnatural circumstances. For Takashi, there was nothing unusual about sleeping for only an hour or so a night. Similarly, he had always been excessively thin, and presently his hollow face resembled his father's more than ever. These conditions that would break most men were painful, certainly, and he would describe them as nothing short of cruel, but he was used to cruelty, and he could tolerate this distress with impenetrable dignity. The memory of that plaintive voice in the darkness saddened him, but it did not haunt him; it was merely another memory that drifted through his mind as the dawn rose, his spirits lifting with it. Meiktila: at least they now had a destination rather than being consigned to loitering around central Burma waiting to be either strafed by low-flying planes or taken down by Gurkhas. Soon, he would forget the corporal's utterance entirely, this recollection of another's distress merging with countless others. Takashi was grateful for having in-herited what others had described as a frigid sort of haughtiness, an "inhuman coldness," as one critic had said of his father, that at times seemed incongruous with his gentle nature. His own suffering was sufficient; adding to it the suffering of others would overburden him. Perhaps his dispassionate, regal bearing, too, served as armor against the frontal assault made by reality. The suffering of the individual he could overcome. Collective suffering would be too much for him to bear, and so he remained detached.

Takashi was an exception, for most of the men found a sort of pur-pose nearing religious ecstasy in this collective suffering, these lives that had been consecrated to the nation being given new purpose in their loyalty to the division. On foreign soil, their existence was vin-dicated by their suffering; fighting for their nation, they found a sense of patriotism that was otherwise unfathomable. In his individualistic way, Takashi understood this. The testament of his doom would be given individual expression.

Takashi rose without having slept.

"Two different voices constantly call to us. One comes from within, the other from without. The one from without is one's daily duty. If the part of the mind that responded to duty corresponded exactly with the voice from within, then one would indeed be supremely happy."

— Yukio Mishima,
Sun and Steel

"One must use the mask of a cause to rule the people. However, having once been used, in the end, the mask of the 'cause' cannot be removed."

— Ryūnosuke Akutagawa,
Shuju no Kotoba

XIV

Outside the Fortress
at Goldland

WAR IS certainly an ugly thing, Takashi thought, but life is filled with many glaring examples of things far more worthy of revulsion. Society, specifically the modern social order that Japan had so hastily begun to adopt less than a century ago, seemed uniquely structured so that only the worst tendencies of human nature were cultivated. Modern Japan was infested with a false sense of patriotism, admirable sentiments having been artificially inflated, he had come to decide, finding the degradation of an otherwise virtuous concept to be distasteful and crass. Meanwhile, the overbearing sentimentalism of those who held that nothing was worth fighting for, that nothing was of sufficient value to warrant military action; those who believed such notions, he wrote off as inflexible cowards. "Heroes have always been monsters who crushed sentimentality underfoot," his father had written in an account of a famed Korean general, an individual soldier, and how the nation is saved from the "evil Japanese" during the reign of King Seonjo. Ryūnosuke had presented the story as a fable, as a semi-historical piece taken from the pages of a mythology book; in his typically dextrous style, he had filled it with bizarre and grotesque imagery such as decapitated bodies, severed limbs, flashing swords... Just the sort of thing Takashi and Hiroshi had enjoyed reading as children. At the end, with a characteristic flourish of irony and wit, their father presented the reader with his critique of such vainglorious stories, claiming that history is filled with tales of triumph for the victors, regardless of the absurd claims of such tales. "To any nation's people, their history is glorious."

The man who holds nothing in such lofty regard as to be willing to fight for it can scarcely be called a man. On the opposite side, the man who regards nothing so sacred as his own comfort, seeking peace at all costs, is a truly pathetic creature, Takashi thought after having seen the acts of heroism undertaken by those around him; those fighting for the enemy he saw as equally heroic. Any man either unable or simply unwilling to recognize this bravery is incapable of knowing freedom unless he is kept free by the force of greater men than he. Previously, he had assumed all men were the same when pushed to their outer limits: any man in any nation in any century. Now it was plainly visible before Takashi's eyes that the opposite was true. Some were simply cowards. These were a wholly distinct breed, a subspecies, if you will, from the brave men who fought either with or against him. As far as he was concerned, no man on either side who had made it this far could be called a coward.

So many of those around him had grown immensely; adolescents had become men, having been witness to a purifying conflagration that those outside their ranks could not fathom. Takashi resented those who spoke of war as representative of nothing worthwhile, only noticing its horrors. Certainly, it was horrible, and the indignities were undeniable, but Takashi had gained, or perhaps earned, certain insights of which he would otherwise have been woefully ignorant. During his twenty-second year of life, he had seen, experienced, and overcome more than had most men twice his age. The men who would survive and return to Japan would do so with a wisdom beyond their years. Perhaps it was his egotism, but Takashi, despite his pain, or perhaps having been made so because of it, was indescribably happy to be alive. He had felt an emotion that he knew his father never had: exhilaration. "My life matters," he thought. "My life matters to me. It matters to my mother, it matters to my brothers, it matters to my nation. Tomorrow, I may die; the day after, I may die, or perhaps my death will occur a month from now. As I now stand, there is no compulsion, there are no orders beyond the duty to fight for all I'm worth." Had he not been conscripted and sent first to Korea and then to Burma, he would never have felt anything with such primal force. At his promotion to First Lieutenant, he felt only gratitude.

Mournfully, even as he felt a certain vain pride, he gazed at his reflection, two bars and two stars having been hastily sewn onto the collar of his threadbare uniform. "The French Officer" so beloved by the Burmese locals was now, indeed, an officer; as was his luck, such a promotion could only occur after another had fallen. Beginning on March 4, 1945, Shōwa 20, the 49th Division, headed by Lieutenant General Saburo Takehara, was directed to advance north in the direction of Meiktila. Their sister regiment, the 168th, had been entirely destroyed after Meiktila had fallen to the 17th Indian Division, the much feared Black Cat Division, largely composed of Gurkha and Sikh regiments. Takashi was presently in charge of the lives of fifty men; having been promoted to this rank due to the death of a brave stranger, he considered the gravity of this. He, with his burgeoning attachment to life, somehow felt gratitude at the prospect of utilizing his death for something greater than himself. It was said that his father beautified his sins with his death; Takashi, then, would weaponize his. A living bullet, indeed, he vowed to better the sergeant's instruction.

Along the roadside could be found Japanese men either too weakened from malaria or too starved to continue. They were indistinguishable from the corpses. "Help a soldier!" one of them would occasionally cry; this meant he expected one of the living to toss him a grenade to end his life. Takashi could not say that he had never aided a man in such a fashion, only that he was still in possession of a grenade.

Once again, politics came to mind. The Japan he so loved was no nation of gods, and the very fact that Takashi so lamented Japan's present corruption forced him to admit his possession of a latent streak of idealism that he fundamentally disliked. "Are we a people who can accomplish nothing resembling self-preservation unless directed to do so by some external force?" The newly christened lieutenant and translator by virtue of his birth asked himself. "Is this how we shall always be? The greatest shame is we don't even regret it. We come up with one argument piled atop yet another ridiculous argument to excuse ourselves… And those arguments we produce in droves! We are fundamentally incapable of distancing ourselves from this pathetic tendency to follow the leader until death. I, too, am guilty of this." An entire nation had been pressed to adopt a uniform mentality, clothing themselves in Western fabrics and Western ideals, and soon the young men of the nation had been fitted with uniforms, scarcely noticing any change at all. These were the model citizens for a dead nation. Now, a people who had never known defeat would soon find themselves at the mercy of those who they so arrogantly imitated. At once, all their faults would be revealed.

The air was sweltering on the broad, grey road whose end was the city gate of Meiktila. Much like his father's famed Rashōmon gate in Kyoto, Takashi imagined it to be surrounded by corpses abandoned by both men and carrion eaters. The soil was cracked; as the heat rose, the road appeared to be coated in a thin layer of ash, and so the rising heat gave the appearance of fragrant smoke. The scent of smoke, too, lingered in the air. Faintly visible in the distance, its stone exterior the color of dry bone, the spire of the Nagayon Temple pierced the sky. The low angle that rose sharply upward before culminating in a pagoda-like summit called to mind the slopes of Mount Fuji. Nearby, the waters of Lake Meiktila reflected the sunlight, shimmering perhaps even more brilliantly in the heat.

A shimmering of heat —
Outside the grave
Alone I dwell.

Along with the poem by Jōsō, quoted by his father shortly before death, memories of the eastern banks of the Sumida River, with those waters the same shade of blue-grey as the glazed tiles of Kyoto, drifted into Takashi's consciousness. As a child, he'd walked along those streets of Honjo with his father and Hiroshi. There was not a single beautiful thing in Honjo, Ryūnosuke had said; not a single beautiful street, even before the earthquake had leveled much of the area... The low-roofed buildings, too, were grey and drab, and the banks of the river were entirely without lustre. The area suggested nothing of the vulgarities of "civilization," apparently; to a four-year-old boy, this was not very interesting. Then, his interest was once again piqued when his father had described the close-cropped head of a corpse bobbing in those waters the color of steel. "A kappa?" he had asked. Then, his father had begun to describe the fishermen in the area, and once again Takashi's interest waned. Still, Ryūnosuke had grown up loving this area, and so Takashi, too, had reflexively loved it. The Ekō-in Temple in Ryōgoku he'd loved especially, treasured even, and Takashi could call to mind memories of those ancient graves and the stone face of the Buddha with startling clarity as he gazed into the depths of Lake Meiktila. As he recalled watching those flowering blossoms of fireworks from the safety of the Ryōgoku bridge, the slate grey waters of Lake Meiktila drifted on as if in perpetuity. Their depths suggested something resembling peace.

Nearby, the red brick buildings had clearly once been quite elegant; at present, along this road lined with dead men and burned-out vehicles, the continental-style villas were shells of what they had once been, shadows of empire. Around them, the flatness of the landscape seemed remarkable, and this was enhanced by the mountains beyond, green and rich; the paradoxical effect verged on obscene.

Meiktila was surely designed by nature as a place to defend. The approaches from the west and from the south were bordered by vast lakes, and so the entryways were, essentially, causeways. Canals and irrigation channels provided a labyrinthine topography, and so the landscape was quite unsuitable for tanks. The same tanks that had so terrified the Japanese on the open planes now faced an entirely different situation in Meiktila. Major General Tomekichi Kasuya and his garrison had, until this week, been firmly entrenched in the lovely town of villas interspersed between tree-lined avenues, determined to fight to the last. Kasuya's elite troops, probably numbering no more than 3,200 in all, these modern incarnations of General Maresuke Nogi's White Sash Brigades, had dug into this terrain entirely unsuitable for tanks, having positioned themselves under houses, in trees, in the banks of the canals…

Few men are by nature brave, but discipline and passion have an uncanny way of inducing this rare force with the capacity to surpass nature. In war, discipline outstrips fury. Their only chance of life was to be found in abandoning all hope of it.

General Slim's rapid onslaught was countered by a stubborn, fatalistic even, Japanese defense from a maze of mutually supported bunkers and the fortified shells of half-burnt houses, using machine guns and anti-tank weapons. The Japanese resistance was fanatical; daring damnation, they frightened the English with the ease in which they cast off their lives. Snipers, though starved, their rifles poorly maintained, picked off infantrymen with daring swiftness as the English and Indians advanced down those tree-lined streets drenched in blinding sunlight. For days, this had continued. Eventually, somehow, tanks were brought in, and street by street, building by building, Meiktila was nearly retaken by the English. Japanese 75-mm guns engaged with English tanks and infantry at point-blank range. The entire town was an enormous series of traps, and still, at the end, only fifty Japanese were left by the third of March. These survivors committed suicide by drowning themselves in Lake Meiktila.

The 49th Division was presently charged with retaking this city so loosely held by the English. Indeed, Japanese flags bleached white by the sun could still be seen draped from certain buildings.

Must the Japanese be made to suffer more? Takashi wondered. "Life is a battle," Ryūnosuke had written in the suicide note especially to his sons. He'd amended it to "Life is a battle culminating in death." Takashi had never before lived with the intent of taking his father's advice so literally. Must the Japanese be pushed down with such merciless force, though? It was as though they'd been shoved down halfway and, suspended without having yet reached the depths of defeat, they rested uneasily at this odd halfway point. This situation was fraught with ambiguities. At least greater suffering, greater losses, would relieve these tedious ambiguities that only served to heighten the already painful tension that hung in the air with the dust. Yes, perhaps greater suffering would inspire greater clarity in their hearts. Once he's had his fill of suffering, any man looks at the world with his eyes wide open. After this, can he not help but be provoked to rage, baring his teeth at this world that has scorned his very existence? Only with this righteous anger, this sublime rage, could any hope for dignity persist under such conditions.

"If we attach no value or do not respect the mental discipline that urges these men to the limits of their endurance, that drives them to advance, there is nothing in this universe, in the heavens or the earth below, that deserves the least respect."

— Sōseki,
The Heredity of Taste

XV

Eyes in Their Last Extremity

IT WAS RUMORED that Tokyo had been bombed flat, but this was entirely unconfirmed; Takashi, with his newly conferred status as an officer, made no mention of this to the platoon of some fifty or so men under his command, nor did he chastise anyone who said such things. To silence them with some terse remark would only serve to further demoralize them. Somehow, all this talk of disaster had the opposite effect. The human psyche is a curious thing: perhaps shifting the focus to the peril of others lifted their spirits. Besides, most of these men were not from Tokyo; few of them had ever even visited Japan's modern capital, and so the burning of Tokyo was scarcely different from the fires presently illuminating Meiktila beneath the dazzlingly white starlight. Fighting had stopped for the night, and still, those fires burned on the horizon. The oil fields, too, blazed in the distance.

Some of the men laughed with friends new and old, and others wept in solitude. No one disturbed them. Some, too, simply stared into the distance, something like anger registering in their eyes even as they said nothing. Even their breath seemed subdued. This anger had been turned inward; they had replaced the external conflict with something excruciatingly, maddeningly internal, and the pain in their eyes saddened Takashi, even as they remained silent. He had been born to feel such existential agony and to bear it with grace. Why had fate seen fit to force such suffering on those so temperamentally unsuited for it? Takashi grieved for their loss of innocence.

Tokyo was burning. Surely his mother had been evacuated to her family's estate in the Kugenuma… Takashi had not heard from Hiroshi in weeks. Yasushi had, indeed, been conscripted. The army likely had little use for pianists at this point, and so Takashi did his best to maneuver his thoughts away from the fate of his brother who had not yet reached twenty. This feat proved to be simple enough, for as per his last correspondence, Hiroshi's second daughter, still a baby, had died. He'd not been there. For all Takashi knew, Hiroshi had been ordered to fly a plane into the deck of some American carrier, perishing hideously in a tangle of twisted metal and flames much like a scene from one of their father's horror novellas.

Takashi had learned to feel anger at the ruinous fates of others even more strongly than he derided his own fate, which he could only regard as dismal. Still, he had no regrets. *I've killed many men*, he thought, recalling Hiroshi's words on November 22, 1943. He would never forget that date. "You will kill men. That much is an inevitability. You are an instrument, the property of the Imperial Japanese Army. Don't think of yourself as a killer. Certainly, you will cause death, but you will bear no more guilt than that rifle they issued to you." Takashi had killed many men, certainly, but he could not say how many men had done their damndest to kill him and failed.

As he began to compose what he assumed would be his final letter, his rifle with that chrysanthemum seal that had been "given to him by the emperor" beside him, Takashi could only contemplate the deaths of others. The prospect of his own death caused him no pain or fear; indeed, he felt a vaguely satisfying emptiness as he contemplated his own demise. Was this what his father felt, this melancholy peace? It was entirely possible that his entire family was dead. At least all of them would know peace, and his brothers would wait to embrace him at the Yasukuni Shrine. His mother would meet as an adult the father whom she had never known, Zengorō Tsukamoto. And Ryūnosuke... Ryūnosuke Akutagawa was no longer tormented. Takashi, too, could die with the satisfaction of knowing that his father had felt only peace in the days leading up to his meticulously staged death. As Takashi composed a letter that he knew would only be read after his death, he found a sense of understanding that most men never reached even after having lived their entire lives.

"To my father..."

Takashi knew quite well that this haiku would be censored, three lines of poetry reduced to three slashes of blue-black ink. His words would be no more than ash. Hiroshi would never read this poem, even if he somehow still lived.

Perhaps the rumor that Tokyo was being bombed was nothing more than a malicious lie spread by the enemy to demoralize these men who were already spiritually and physically impoverished. Even if Tokyo was razed, though, surely the city would eventually recover. The great Kanto earthquake had leveled the city the year after Takashi's birth, and yet he had not grown up in a ruined city. Tokyo could certainly recover; once again, Tokyo could be remade, even from the lowest depths. Even without the bombings, the situation in Tokyo was surely dismal, but Takashi had seen in its denizens the refinement of a people who had been forced to bear the meagerness of their daily lives by cultivating a taste for simplicity. These people who counted the baroque as vice and paucity as virtue could certainly recover from even the cruelest punishment the enemy, in this case, the Americans, he assumed, could inflict upon them. Tokyo was resilient, if nothing else... Still, he felt a certain hatred burning within him as he imagined the skyline of Tokyo ablaze. Surely, someone would protect his mother?

The censors had done their best to conceal this, but it was clear that the poverty in both rural and urban Japan had long since surpassed the point of being considered virtuous. In a word, people were starving. The war had transformed this paucity of resources into a cancer, the worst sort of evil, a spiritual void stripped of all beauty or any meaningful sense of expression. Takashi knew from the depths of his heart that from this desolation would spring a new sort of art; from this scorched earth would be borne a new art, a new beauty, liberated from the shackles of the past and yet too fainthearted to risk flying too near the blinding sun. Much would be gained, but something ethereal, some ineffable quality would be lost. Regardless, Takashi knew he would not be around to see the results. In a frenzy, he wrote. Now everyone around him slept, but Takashi wrote on ever more furiously, as he'd seen his father do in one of his fits of artistic fury. It would all be censored, all of it, he knew, and so he continued to write these words that would soon have no meaning, only to be seen by the eyes of the dead.

The black lines of the censors... These would not stand between Takashi and his destiny. He and each of these men who had fallen into the pervasive darkness of sleep from either sheer exhaustion or the calm held in the peace conferred by the certainty of a ruinous present, all of these men had sacrificed much to arrive at this point, this Rubicon they would shortly cross. All of these souls, battered and yet unbeaten; victorious in the cold certainty of their defeat. Yes, this was surely what his father had known on the night of July 23, 1927, the year following the death of the Taishō Emperor. These men knew something beyond flesh, beyond blood. They had come to know something beyond the present and had chosen to press forward towards an uncertain fate that could only end in their demise. If they believed in nothing but their own mortal lives, they would not have found such strength. By now, all of them had been witness to events that anyone who had not seen combat would deem as supernatural. From these events, they derived courage beyond the hearts of mortals. Their ears rang with the sounds of mortars and shrieks of pain and rattles of death; their eyes were bloodshot and weary. Even so, they carried on. Even after witnessing the torments of despair beyond death, they carried on, lightning in their hearts. Nothing could stand between them and eternity. Oh, certainly, this would all be censored, but damn it all! To hell with the censors! History served as a reminder that these men had reached a state beyond flesh and blood. In his mind, Takashi had surpassed all of this. Yes, this fire in his heart, this insatiable flame, in this, Takashi knew his father's mental landscape immediately before his death, and, oh, it was glorious.

Only the dawn could halt his writing. Time had deserted him, and only the shadows of thoughts remained. Meiktila was in flames, and Takashi's heart was in flames. His spirit had been burnished by the flames of all the souls who had perished before him. So many had died while still he lived; many had suffered for his survival, and he was so, so grateful for the opportunity to do right by the brave souls of these beautiful dead. As the sun rose, he refused to extinguish the flames of hope kindled by the sacrifices of all of those who had perished before him. The cruel winds, try as they may, would be powerless to snuff this flame that still raged within his heart. "I am worthy, I am worthy," he thought, too proud to weep even as he gasped for breath.

None among them were cowards; none among them were fear-mongers or deserters. These men were fearless. The order had been given to fight until the death.

"You will all surely die, but even so, know this: in death, you will win this battle."

Even as he heard this order, Takashi knew it to be a brazen lie. This battle would certainly be lost. The entire war, too, would be lost, he assumed. Regardless, he was not discouraged. He had fought bravely, and there was no room in his heart for discouragement. He would go to his death without fear; under no circumstances would he withdraw. Survival would amount to defeat. He would not remain among the living in Burma, and so he would take his place among the deceased. He would go into this final battle accompanied by the souls of innumerable martyrs, countless ancestors who had died in glory.

The sky that day was much like the human mind, with uncannily shifting images and caverns and vast heights, filled with strange mists and lakes of blue as radiant as eternity, and the bright illumination of those forgotten memories… Sunlight, illusions, mysteries, thunderheads hinting at spring rain, in all of it, smoke like opium swirled around them as they went through horrors that had by now become routine during those hellish days, seeing visions of death after having been molded into the dealers of death. The wasteland stretched beyond them as though endless, a desert of the soul, and their tragedy was not that they could not see it, but that they could see all too much of it. Within them, too, was a desolate stretch of violent emptiness. "The Wasteland grows; woe to those who cannot see the wastelands within," Nietzsche wrote. With practiced ease, Takashi used those tightly constrained flames of that vast and burning emptiness within to scorch this hellscape that had formed around him. This constant barrage of shelling, these machine guns pounding away like some rainstorm clashing within the depths of the earth, in the midst of all of this, some of the men behaved as though in a state of hypnosis, charging forward with either bayonets or sharpened bamboo poles before twitching backwards, shot, falling heavily to the ground beneath violent sprays of blood that gleamed like a hail of rubies beneath the sunlight. It was all so obscene, so grotesque; how many of them even realized they were dying? Delirious, perhaps it was kinder that they died with their eyes unclouded by fear, seeing only the glory known to heroes and lunatics within their final moments.

They'd been told not to use their grenades unless they encountered tanks. At present, they were under siege by both English and American tanks, and grenades were in short supply, much like bullets. The officers fought on with their swords.

The mutilated corpses surrounding them had ceased to have any semblance of meaning except to serve as omnipresent symbols of the outward manifestation of death itself. It was impossible to move without stumbling over the tangled limbs of the dead and dying, some of them to weak or injured even to cry out; others begged to be killed. Certain fates were truly worse than death. Some of the living moved as though having been blinded, entranced; these unhuman battlefield experiences had made permeable the boundary delineating reality and the moonlit realm of dreams, of terrifying visions seen only in nightmares, this merging of the living and the dead. Bullets tore through the air and scarred the walls of the burned-out red brick villa behind which they sheltered, poorly shielded from those with vastly superior armaments. In the distance, Takashi could see a tank positioned beneath the shade of a large flowering palm whose branches had been all but shredded by artillery. He felt as though he'd lived through this entire day before, again and again in endless repetition, this ceaseless sequence of motion; in short, he felt himself to be no more of a living thing than that tank beneath the narrow shadow, that contemptible machine designed with the express purpose of causing death. He was the record of a living being. In this, he differed little from the corpses, and still he persisted. Even in his delirium, he continued on with the blind fury of instinct, repeatedly enacting memories that soon left him without a trace of having ever existed in the first place.

"These sightless eyes give me no pain..."

A better shot than most, Takashi continued firing, and the scarce bullets were put to good use when entrusted to this mild-mannered lieutenant, even as his psyche was shattered and a strange feeling of unreality clouded his vision. So, this was what his father saw... The landscape that made itself so painfully, exquisitely clear before his eyes as he fired off round after round more resembled a painting than anything of this world; indeed, it could have been painted in cruel relief by Goya. It was as though a spirit hovered behind each bullet, each slug of lead possessing a volition of its own, just as alive and vital as its target. Death made its presence visible in all of its myriad of agonizing forms. On the ground, limbless bodies continued to be riddled with bullets, recoiling when hit as though still living. Reality was subverted. This effect was especially tragic when the faces remained recognizably human, the eyes still open as though held so by copper wire. Eventually, most of those faces ceased to resemble anything that had ever lived.

Some men had begun to be picked off ahead of him, and so Takashi could only assume the enemy would soon smash through these walls that had been weakened to the point of breaking, bringing him irrevocably into the fray. He was out of bullets... Rather than feeling anything resembling fear, he was furious. Around him, the American, English, and now Indian artillery continued to thunder, and the very earth seemed to rattle beneath his feet, threatening to throw him off balance and into that perverse tangle of gore that painted the soil a vivid crimson. Indeed, the ground may well have been a swamp. Fixing his eyes upon that tank that appeared to be split in two by the slim and narrow shadow of the stripped palm, with his teeth he pulled the pin from a grenade and hurled it with an overhand motion in an arching trajectory. For a second, he heard nothing, his eyes reducing all to silence as they followed that small thing gleaming silver beneath the sun. It landed beneath the tank, rolling for an instant before exploding in a blinding flash of white hot light.

"Banzai! Banzai!"

They would lose, that much was certain, and still the destruction of this lone target gave them no small measure of satisfaction. These cries betrayed no sentimentality; no trite recitation of love for the emperor or the beauty of sacrifice for Yamato were spoken, and so only the battle cries of these delirious men could be heard, startling in their purity. There was not a trace of bitterness in their shouts. These cries were meaningless; these individual expressions of ecstasy at one small victory in a battle which would surely lead to death were nothing if not glorious.

More men soon came to join the ranks of their fallen comrades, husks emptied of any semblance of life. Endless streams of shells, their own and those of the enemy, passed overhead with a shrill, nearly whining rush, as though having no greater substance than the air itself... As soon as these shells landed, though, with those explosions that may well have been supernatural, their existence was verified in the ensuing carnage, meteoric in destruction. The midday sun radiated from above, both abrasive and obliquely indirect as the sounds of mortars split the heavens.

It did not occur to Takashi to seek out any avenue of escape; he could see no salvation, and this caused him no fear. Beyond this, the lack of any prospect of survival only served to embolden him. Now without bullets, armed with his bayonet and his sword, he was prepared to strike at anyone who might come at him. He was hopeless, certainly, but far from helpless. Hand-to-hand combat commenced, and he brought down his opponents without distress. These actions, these vicious strikes, were not the result of any conscious process of thought, but rather the purity of instinct that was the result of both intense strength of mind and the finesse present only after years of training. He fought as though having entered a tiger's den. Above, bright wisps of cloud streaked the sky as swords, bayonets, and sharpened bamboo sticks collided with human flesh. Even as this frenetic maelstrom continued, one man after another continued to be cut down by artillery.

Takashi had survived into the present only because the blood of other men had been spilled. The universe in which he existed had been reduced to nothing beyond his ability to strike; in other words, he was reduced to pure function, and so he was no longer confined to that mirrored prison of the mind that had so relentlessly tormented him in the past. Liberated from either thought or hope, he no longer saw his father's visions of hell. Takashi had no recollection of his life before Meiktila; such reflections were presently stripped of all value or emotion. His existence was verified only in this ability to act. In this state of detachment was a sort of serenity that he had previously found incomprehensible. Now, many times, he had seen all hope or despair or, indeed, sense itself, leave a man's eyes. In each instance, his existence was verified; the cessation of the heartbeat of another gave veracity to his own existence.

Existence had become tiresome. In a very primal sort of way, requiring no thought, Takashi had grown weary; for the first time in his life, this was a weariness entirely without introspection that presently enveloped him. So this was what his father had felt after having taken "those pills…" Bathed in sunlight, he remained unblinking as his sword cut down one man after another; after each strike, he retreated behind the safety of that red brick wall that had by now been nearly annihilated. He was no longer conscious even of his own breathing, which had grown quite rapid, and without thought or calculation, his mind focused on the barely perceptible changes in the postures of his opponents, those subtle shifts in their stances betraying weaknesses which he could use to his advantage. Again and again, he struck.

As one might expect, undernourished and weakened by exhaustion, Takashi's mental state that had been near enlightenment soon departed only to nourish that void within with newfound aches and pains, and visions of the hellscape that stretched on before him had once again begun to register in his consciousness. In the periphery of his line of sight, he saw the faces of those dead men who were by now as close to him as Hiroshi or Yasushi. Like sparks emanating from the rapid strikes of his sword, from time to time those faces flashed in his mind, both vivid and melancholy. As rapidly as these thoughts would appear, the incontrovertible reality of death right before his eyes would in the same moment extinguish any such meaningless thoughts. He now had no use for thoughts without meaning. Like the interminable beating of countless wings, the sounds of artillery and the cries of men persisted. Takashi relied on his lack of all fear of death in these moments. There were perhaps twenty Japanese men left alive within his field of vision.

Once again deprived of thought in a state of exacerbated delirium, did he secretly yearn for something beyond this? Those tapered and narrow fingers, so like the elegant hands of his father; were these hands meant to be stained with blood; were these hands meant to kill? His father's hands had only been stained with ink… Before him now was a field of darkness, a void. Was there no end to this? This cruel expanse, was this eternity? If the inviolable truth of his existence had ceased to be valid, then this life was, indeed, pointless, and yet the dignity of his spirit deprived him of the option to simply close his eyes and breathe no more. Such an existence was agonizing. Living like this was painful beyond belief.

He began to feel something that was surely impossible to grasp by one in an otherwise lucid state of mind… All at once, this vague sense of anxiety left him.

Takashi only realized he'd been shot by the damp crimson that had begun to spread across the front of his uniform. He was not at all startled, nor was he horrified; the feeling was that of a sudden impact which somehow lacked any sort of vivid sensation. This was clarity; this was purity, eternity. For two years, he had awaited this thing called death that was now stirring echoes of something quite ancient in his mind. This distortion of physical and emotional sensation was beyond description. "So, this is death…" It was surreal. Now, his chest burned; he was certain he cried out even as he could not recall it. Everything had begun to grow dim. Around him, sounds emanated from in-discernible, indescribable sources as flashes of light illuminated the darkness; some were human voices, certainly, in English and Japanese, and the faces of men smeared with blood and sweat disappeared only to reassert themselves to the exclusion of all else. The world had been thrust aside into relativity, into meaningless abstraction, and now only time was moving. Soon he came to feel a pervasive sense of peace, a rose-suffused comprehension of eternity. All of the horrors and petty indignities of the previous two years left his memory. Something like blindness, or perhaps sleep, pleasantly began to overwhelm him, and as his legs collapsed beneath him, momentum brought Takashi to the ground that had earlier seemed so unsteady. He saw not the sky; he saw not the blood-drenched panorama that stretched on so endlessly; nor was he burned by the glare of the sun above. What he saw was but a vast, limitless night. Above, the sun blazed on in cloudless cruelty, its rays illuminating only the vivid darkness of death.

Author's Afterword

Takashi Akutagawa died on Friday, April 13, 1945, in the Yamethin district during the aftermath of the Battle of Meiktila. In an especially cruel twist of fate, on the same day his mother's home was destroyed during the firebombing of Tokyo. His older brother, Hiroshi Akutagawa, survived the war to became an actor, translator, and director most noteworthy for his performance as Hamlet; his younger brother, Yasushi Akutagawa, also survived, becoming one of the most famous composers in Japan. Takashi Akutagawa's posthumous Buddhist name is Ichijoin Seichu Hidaka.

In Michio Takeyama's novel *The Burmese Harp*, the hero, Private Mizushima, survives, disappearing into the heart of Burma as a Buddhist monk. While fully acknowledging that Takashi Akutagawa perished in Meiktila, the author would like to imagine that Takashi lived on much like the fictitious Mizushima.

Completed Wednesday, April 13, 2022.

ALSO FROM LEGEND BOOKS

Aelita by Alexei Tolstoy

The Fate of Homo Sapiens by H. G. Wells

The New World Order by H. G. Wells

Early Days of World History by Oswald Spengler

The Hour of Decision by Oswald Spengler

Man and Technics by Oswald Spengler

Prussianism and Socialism by Oswald Spengler

Empire in Apocalypse by Robert Bruton

www.ingramcontent.com/pod-product-compliance
Lightning Source LLC
Chambersburg PA
CBHW030326160726
47992CB00005B/2182